O P D - I

What All African Americans Need to Know

By

Gosby King Jr., EdD

Copyright © 2016

Oppression Personality Disorder-I: What All African Americans Need to Know

Library of Congress Catalog Card Number
TXU 1-740-766

ISBN: 978-0-9848126-0-8
ISBN: 0984812601

Published by
Gosby King Jr., EdD
Dallas, Texas

Cover concept by Doug Duncan

The names used in case examples are fictitious and any resemblance
to actual persons living or dead is entirely coincidental.

Printed in the United States of America

Contents

Dedication and Acknowledgments

I would like to acknowledge and dedicate this book to the following persons:

To my maternal grandfather, Robert L. Thomas, who taught me to live without fear and compromise.

To my paternal grandfather, Huey King, who taught me patience and the value of silence.

To my father, Gosby King Sr., MA, who challenged me to be more.

To Robert L. Ware, PhD, the first African-American psychologist I was exposed to and mentored by, for providing lessons in discipline and focus.

To Edison R. Fowlks, PhD, who provided encouragement and friendship.

To Robert L. Williams, PhD, who challenged my sensibilities and provided an opportunity to grow and to develop.

To R. Paul Johnson, EdD, who also challenged and encouraged me.

To my many mothers who nurtured and shaped my life: Cora L. King, Pearl L. Thomas, Verdie L. Marshall, and Margarita A. King.

To my wife, Shirley Wesley King, PhD; my daughter, Melanie M. King; my son, Wesley M. King; my granddaughter, Lourdes M. Queen; and my granddaughter, Haley V. Brown, all of whom have had to live with me as I have pursued my obsession.

To my brother Huey J. King and my nephew Huey J. King, Jr., my late sister Vera J King and her son Jansen King Sherman, Shelia, Robbie, Victor, Bruce, Ora, Cora, Elzora and all others that have touched my life.

...emancipate yourselves from mental
slavery, none but ourselves can free
our minds...

—Bob Marley
"Redemption Song"

Introduction

After thirty-five years of studying and practicing psychotherapy with African-American clients, I have been compelled to write about my observations and experiences. I believe it was my destiny and my purpose to bring to light or add to the understanding of the psychological conditions that continue to oppress African Americans in the United States. There has been great reluctance by African Americans to discuss what they consider to be the most intimate aspects of the African-American community and culture; this reluctance is akin to exposing the "family secret" to outsiders, who may then judge and ridicule an already sensitive and fragile existence. Like the family secret, everybody already knows about it, and everyone has agreed not to openly discuss the horrible family secret because of the shame, fear, and anger associated with it. I believe the grave circumstances facing the African-American community demand that African Americans cry out. After 465 years of slavery and oppression, the African-American community is experiencing a multitude of concerns, many of which have reached the point of crisis. These concerns involve generally low self-regard; the loss of group identity; high rates of incarceration, school dropouts, drug abuse/addiction, teenage pregnancy, AIDS, and unemployment; and the erosion of basic essential values that shape and strengthen individuals, family, and the community. Post-1964, with the passing of the Civil Rights Act (discussed below), African-American communities have experienced a general reversal of forward progress in many areas. African Americans have to move forward to the next level of independence, which is economic self-sufficiency. Many of the problems and concerns the African-American community faces will not be resolved through legislation, politics, or protest: African Americans themselves must directly address the internal issues that hinder economic progress. If the internal issues of the African-American community are to be resolved, then they have to be addressed internally and within the African-American community itself. The solutions to these problems and issues will require introspection (self-evaluation) by each and every African American.

Introspection is imperative if African Americans are to move forward to the next level of liberation. In other words, African Americans must look inwardly to find the solution—to look within themselves, to look at their communities, to look at their overall situation and circumstances—in order to correct many of the issues and problems they face today. Many of the problems African Americans face will be solved and resolved by African Americans correcting themselves. Many of the issues that confront African Americans today were born of and created by years of slavery and legalized oppression of freedom and personal rights. African Americans' ancestors were captives of a slave system that was created to produce wealth and comfort for whites. The Willie Lynch system and Jim Crow laws, and the residual customs of those laws, have maintained racism and discrimination that help to insure that African Americans remain dysfunctional and oppressed to this day. African Americans have been psychologically oppressed for over 465 years as of this writing. Because of this psychological oppression, African Americans have become self-destructive in many aspects of their lives. African Americans have found themselves entangled in a web of devaluation and disenfranchisement. Future generations of African Americans will continue to carry out this human self-destruction and self-debasement unless a clearly defined strategic plan is implemented to reverse this trend of oppression-related behavior. Abram Kardiner and Lionel Ovesey describe the effects of slavery and oppression in their 1951 book *The Mark of Oppression*. The first step in devising a solution is therefore to help African Americans become aware of the exact nature of the many problems associated with long-term psychological and physical oppression.

Let it be clear that African Americans have come a long way in overcoming the effects of slavery and oppression. Given the circumstances they have had to deal with, it is miraculous and a testimony to the human spirit that some African Americans have been able to survive and endure as well as they have. While some African Americans are doing fairly well, the majority when examined using the typical social indicators are not doing so well. Subscribing to the old adage that "until the lowliest among us is raised, we all remain oppressed," those few cannot claim success until those at the bottom of the well are also liberated. African Americans must learn to acknowledge and embrace one another in their common plight. As long as African Americans as a people disregard one another and fail to find common ground and mutuality in their existence, African Americans will continue to sustain the oppressor's power and control over them.

This book is aimed at shocking the consciousness and stirring African Americans from complacency to action. It is intended to be a beacon and to serve as a kind of lighthouse that African Americans can follow in their quest for complete freedom that can only be achieved through healthy psychological well-being. I am sure you are aware of the purpose of a lighthouse. A lighthouse is used to guide ships during the night or during poor weather conditions when visibility is minimal. The purpose of a lighthouse is to help the ships stay on the correct path and to help them avoid running aground and crashing into rocks or reefs. Without a lighthouse, many ships that travel in the dark could not successfully find their way. The lighthouse has come to play an important role in ensuring the safe and successful passage of ships on their journeys. I hope this book will serve as a kind of lighthouse for African Americans on their journey out of psychological darkness by stimulating self-examination, self-correction, and self-healing in the effort to undo the tremendous psychological damage African Americans have suffered for centuries now.

Like the underground railroad, I hope that by discussing and examining the behavioral and psychological effects of slavery and oppression, African Americans can be guided to a new and complete freedom through psychological healing. By understanding the nature of the problem, African Americans can then fashion a solution and a remedy for the pain and the wounds that all African Americans share. African Americans must reestablish what has been lost and what has been deliberately taken from them—their freedom, dignity, and wealth. The struggle for African Americans today is no longer for physical freedom or political freedom: African Americans' great, determined, and persevering ancestors have already provided their descendants with these. African Americans must now complete the struggle by attending to their psychological well-being. To put it another way, African Americans must engage in psychological recovery from the damage caused by slavery and oppression. African Americans must first understand their purpose as individuals; then they must understand their purpose as a collective. Once African Americans truly understand this, then they can understand that their purpose as individuals is intricately connected to that of the collective group. African Americans have to recognize that as a people they have been dysfunctional in several areas. Once they understand the nature of their dysfunction or psychological illness, then they can engage in self-healing. This book is therefore akin to a road map that points the way toward the healing process; by using this map, African Americans can assume their just and proper place in America that has already been established and paid for, several times over, by previous generations of African Americans. It is the responsibility of each generation to assume their rightful place in the struggle in order to sustain and elevate themselves and African American culture to a higher level of functioning.

The purpose of this book is twofold. The first purpose is to examine and discuss the dysfunctional behaviors of African Americans and how these behaviors are directly related to the experiences of slavery and oppression. In order to understand the effects of slavery and oppression, this book will introduce and discuss a new personality disorder—one I call "oppression personality disorder-I" (OPD-I)—that defines and explains the dysfunctional behaviors of African Americans. The manifestations of OPD-I will be examined on several different levels. The analysis of OPD-I will begin at the individual level. The examination explores how OPD-I is expressed in different areas of African-American life such as in interpersonal relationships, in couples and marriages, in families, and in child rearing. A discussion of OPD-I at the collective level will be conducted by examining African-American organizations.

The second purpose of this book is to teach African Americans how to reprogram themselves and how to eliminate the limiting and dysfunctional behaviors associated with OPD-I. This book is also intended as a guide and a reference for African-American professionals in the areas of social and behavioral sciences: counselors, psychologists, marriage and family therapists, psychiatrists, social workers, and educators, among others. It is imperative that African-American social and behavioral practitioners become aware and understand the exact nature of the elements that affect the emotional lives of African Americans; then, they must develop the skills to optimally assist African-American clients to achieve their highest and best mental-health status possible. African-American practitioners will have to begin with themselves first if they want to eliminate their own areas of dysfunction as they relate to OPD-I. The movement toward psychological healing will be accomplished by understanding the significance of African-American history and the role it plays in defining purpose for African Americans. Armed with an understanding of history, African Americans can then begin to correct or reprogram their thoughts and behaviors in a more productive way. They can strategically define the purpose in their lives and direct their energy, efforts, and talents toward personal, family, community, and societal optimization.

In order for African Americans to correct their psychological processes and to begin to move toward psychological health and productivity, it will be vital to understand how African Americans were transformed into adopting the slave mentality. To help establish this basis of understanding, the book will thus present the "Willie Lynch Letter" as a part of this work. While many African Americans have heard of the Willie Lynch Letter (henceforth "WLL"), few have read it for themselves. Therefore, I believe that a reading of the WLL is a necessary first step to understanding the perspective of this book and its intended purpose of offering a solution to correcting the effects of psychological slave programming. This book is intended to clarify the willful inhumanity and the willful design of destruction from which a cleverly orchestrated plan was put in place to strip African Americans of their sense of humanity, collective identity, and higher calling. Establishing this context will create the basis for understanding what this book seeks to accomplish.

Chapter I: The Business of Slavery

The Willie Lynch Letter: Fact or Fiction?

Some people whom I have encountered want to dismiss the WLL as inauthentic: something with little if any credibility. My more intellectual acquaintances want references and other documentation. I will admit that I have not sought to identify any references for the letter or its origins; I believe others have already accomplished this task. I personally accept the letter as being authentic. Whether or not the letter is authentic, the prescriptions outlined for making a slave out of the African are sound in both theory and technique. The only authentication I believe is necessary is one anecdotal thing. I ask skeptical people one question: "What was the hanging of a black person referred to or called?" After some brief thought, everyone whom I have asked the question has responded with variations of the same answer: "They call it a lynching." So why was the hanging of a black person referred to as "a lynching" and not simply "a hanging"? The hanging of the African slave was referred to as a "lynching" because hanging was a specific method of control taught by Willie Lynch. The hanging of a black person was referred to as a "lynching" because hanging a black person was a prescribed method of controlling slaves by instilling fear within them. If a slave was too difficult to deal with and was rebellious, the rebellious slave would be tortured and hanged while the other slaves were forced to watch. The hanging of a slave was therefore referred to as a "lynching" because the purpose of the hanging was to maintain psychological control over the slaves. It is the use of the term "lynching" that validates the authenticity of the WLL for me. Whether the WLL is factual or not—and I believe it is—the content of the letter certainly describes the treatment of the enslaved African in America. African Americans must understand the slave-socialization process in order to understand the basis for much of the dysfunctional behavior we currently observe among African Americans. The effects of slavery and long-term oppression can be observed in the thoughts and behaviors of African Americans today, just as Willie Lynch predicted. I will let you be the judge of the authenticity of the WLL by having you read it for yourself.

The Willie Lynch Letter

The following message was delivered by a white slave owner named William "Willie" Lynch on the banks of the James River of Virginia in 1712. Any spelling, grammatical, and punctuation errors have been left as is; the italics have been added for emphasis.

Gentlemen, I greet you here on the banks of the James River in the year of our Lord one thousand seven hundred and twelve. First, I shall thank you, the gentlemen of the Colony of Virginia for bringing me here. I am here to help you solve some of your problems with slaves. Your invitation reached me on my modest plantation in the West Indies where I have experimented with some of the newest and still the oldest methods for control of slaves. Ancient Rome would envy us if my program is implemented. As our boat sailed south on the James River, named for our Illustrious King, whose version of the Bible we cherish, I saw enough to know that your problem is not unique. While Rome used cords of wood as crosses for standing human bodies along its old highways in great numbers, you are here using tree and the rope on occasion.

   I caught the whiff of a dead slave hanging from a tree a couple of miles back. You are not only losing valuable stock by hangings, you are having uprisings, slaves are running away, your crops are sometimes left in the field too long for maximum profit, you suffer occasional fires, and your animals are being killed. Gentlemen, you know what your problems are; I do not need to elaborate. I am not here to enumerate your problems; however, I am here to introduce you to a method of solving them.

   In my bag here, I have a foolproof method for controlling your Black slaves. I guarantee every one of you that if installed correctly, it will control the slaves for at least 300 years. My method is simple. Any member of your family or your overseer can use it.

I have outlined a number of *differences* among the slaves, and I take these differences and make them bigger, I use *fear, distrust, and envy* for control purposes. These methods have worked on my modest plantation in the West Indies and it will work throughout the South. Take this simple little list of differences, and think about them. On top of my list is "age" but it is there only because it starts with an "A"; the second is "color" or shade, there is intelligence, size, sex, size of plantations, status on plantation, attitude of owners, whether the slaves lives in the valley, on the hill, East, West, North, South, have fine hair, course hair, or is tall or short. Now that you have a list of differences, I shall give you an outline of action—but before that I shall assure you that distrust is stronger that trust, and envy is stronger than adulation, respect, or admiration. The Black slave after receiving this indoctrination shall carry on and will become self-refueling and self-generating for hundreds of years, maybe thousands. Don't forget you must pitch the old black male vs. the young black male and the young black male against the old black male. You must use the dark skin slaves vs. the light skin slaves and the light skin slaves against the dark skin slaves. You must use the female vs. male, and the male vs. the female. You must also have your white servants and overseers Distrust all Blacks, but it is necessary that your slaves trust and depend on us. They must love, respect and trust only us. Gentlemen, these kits are your keys to control. Use them. Have your wives and children use them, never miss an opportunity. If used intensively for one year, the slaves themselves will remain perpetually distrustful. "Let's Make a Slave" is a study of the scientific process of man breaking and slave making. It describes the rationale and results of the Anglo Saxon's ideas and methods of insuring the master/slave relationship.

The Origin and Development of a Social Being Called the Negro

Let us make a slave a slave. What do I need? First of all we need a Black nigger man, a pregnant nigger woman and her baby nigger boy. Second, I will use the same basic principle that we use in the breaking of a horse, combined with some more sustaining factors. When we do it with horses we break them from one form of life to another; that is, we reduce them from their natural state in nature; whereas nature provides them with the natural capacity to take of their needs and the needs of their offspring, we break that natural string of independence from them and thereby create a dependency state so that we may be able to get from them useful production for our business and pleasure.

Cardinal Principles for Making a Slave

For fear that out future generations may not understand these principles of braking both horses and men, we lay down the art. For, if we are to sustain our basic economy we must break and tie both of the beasts together, the nigger and the horse. We understand the short range planning in economics result in periodic economic chaos; so that, to avoid turmoil in the economy, it requires us to have breadth and depth in long range comprehensive planning, articulating both skills and sharp perception.

We lay down the following principles for long range comprehensive economic planning:

1) Both horse and nigger are no good to the economy in the wild or natural state.

2) Both must be broken and tied together for orderly production.

3) For the orderly futures, special and particular attention must be paid to the female and the young offspring.

4) Both must be crossbred to produce a variety and division of labor.

5) Both must be taught to respond to a particular new language.

6) Mental and physical instruction of containment must be created for both.

We hold the above six cardinal principles as true to be self-evident, based on the following discourse concerning the economics of breaking and tying the horse and the nigger together—all inclusive of the six principles laid down above.

NOTE: Neither principle alone will suffice for good economics. All principles must be employed for the orderly good of the nation.

Accordingly, both a wild horse and a wild or a natural nigger is dangerous even if captured for they will have a tendency to seek their customary freedom, and, in doing so, might kill you in your sleep. You cannot rest. They sleep while you are awake and are awake while you are sleep. They are dangerous near the family house and it requires too much labor to watch them away from the house. Above all you cannot get them to work in the natural state. Hence, both the horse and the nigger must be broken, that is break them from one form of mental life to another—keep the body and take the mind. In other words, break the will to resist. Now the breaking process is the same for both the nigger and the horse, only slightly varying in degrees. But as we said before, there is an art in long-range economic planning. You must keep your eye and thoughts on the female and the offspring of the horse and the nigger.

A brief discourse in offspring development will shed light on the key to sound economic principles. Pay little attention to the generation of original breaking but concentrate on future generations. Therefore, if you break the female mother, she will break the offspring in its early years of development and when the offspring is old enough to work, she will deliver it up to you for her normal female protective tendencies will have been lost in the original breaking process.

For example, take the case of the wild stud horse, a female horse and an already infant horse, and compare the breaking process with two captured nigger males in their natural state, a pregnant nigger woman with her infant offspring. Take the stud horse, break him from limited containment. Completely break the female horse until she becomes very gentle whereas you or anybody can ride her in comfort. Breed the mare and the stud until you have the desired offspring. Then you can turn the stud to freedom until you need him again. Train the female horse whereby she will eat out of your hand, and she will in turn train the infant horse to eat out of your hand also. When it comes to breaking the uncivilized nigger, use the same process, but vary the degree and step up the pressure so as to do a complete reversal of the mind. Take the meanest and most restless nigger, strip him of his clothes in front of the remaining male niggers, the female, and the nigger infant, tar and feather him, tie each leg to a different horse in opposite directions, set him afire, and beat both horses to pull him apart in front of the remaining niggers. The next step is to take a bull whip and beat the remaining nigger male to the point of death in front of the female and the infant. Don't kill him, but *put the fear of God in him, for he can be useful for future breeding.*

The Breaking Process of the African Woman

Then take the female, run a series of tests on her to see if she will submit to your desires willingly. Test her in every way because she is the most important factor for good economics. If she shows any sign of resistance in submitting completely to your will, do not hesitate to bullwhip on her to extract the last bit of bitch out of her. Take care not to kill her, for, in doing so, you spoil good economics. When in complete submission, she will train her offspring in the early years to submit to labor when they become of age. Understanding is the best thing. Therefore, we shall go deeper into this area of the subject matter concerning what we have produced here in this breaking process of the female nigger. We have reversed the relationships. In her natural uncivilized state she would have a strong dependency on the uncivilized nigger male, and she would have a limited protective tendency toward her independent male offspring and would raise the female offspring to be dependant like her. Nature had intended for this type of balance.

We reverse nature by burning and pulling one civilized nigger apart and bull whipping the other to the point of death— all in their presence. By her being left alone, unprotected, with the male image destroyed, the ordeal caused her to move from her psychological dependant state to a frozen independent state. *In this frozen psychological state of independence she will raise her male and female offspring in reversed roles. For fear of the young male's life, she will psychologically train him to be mentally weak and dependent but physically strong. Because she has become psychologically independent, she will train her female offspring to be psychologically independent. What have you got?* You've got the nigger woman out front and the man behind and scared. This is the perfect situation for sound sleep and economics.

Before the breaking process, we had to be alertly on guard at all times. Now we can sleep soundly, for out of frozen fear, his woman stands guard for us. He cannot get past her infant slave process. *He is a good tool; now ready to be tied to a horse at a tender age.*

By the time a nigger boy reaches the age of sixteen, he is soundly broken in and ready for life's sound and efficient work and the reproduction of a unit of good labor force. Continually, through the breaking of uncivilized savage niggers, by throwing the nigger female savage into a frozen psychological state of independency, by killing of the protective male image creating a submissive dependent mind of the nigger male savage, we have created an orbiting cycle that turns in its own axis forever, unless a phenomenon occurs and reshifts the positions of the female savages. We show what we mean by example. Take the case of the two economic slave units and examine them closely.

The Negro Marriage Unit

We breed two nigger males and two nigger females. Then we take the nigger males from them and keep them moving and working. Say the one nigger female bears a nigger female and the other bears a nigger male. Both nigger females, being without the influence of the nigger image, frozen with an independent psychology, will raise her offspring into reverse positions. The one with the female offspring will teach her to be like herself, independent and negotiable (we negotiate with her, through her, by her, and negotiate her at will). The one with the nigger male offspring, she being frozen with a subconscious fear for his life, will raise him to be mentally dependent and weak, but physically strong—in other words, body over mind. Now in a few years when these two offspring become fertile for reproduction, we will mate and breed them and continue the cycle. That is good, sound, and long range comprehensive planning.

Warning: Possible Interloping Negatives

Earlier, we talked about the non-economic good of the horses and the nigger in their wild or natural state: We talked about principle of breaking and tying them together for orderly production. Furthermore, we talked about paying particular attention to the female savage and her offspring for orderly future planning; then, more recently we stated that, by reversing the positions of the male and female savages, we had created an orbiting cycle that turns in its own axis forever, until this phenomenon occurred and reshifted the positions of the male and female savages.

Our experts warned us about the possibility of the phenomenon occurring, for they say the mind has a strong drive to correct and recorrect itself over a period of time. If it can touch a substantial original historic base; and they advised us that the best way to deal with the phenomenon is to shave off the brute's mental history and create a multiplicity of phenomena of illusions that each illusion will twirl in its own orbit, something similar to floating balls in a vacuum. This creation of multiplicity of phenomena of illusions entails the principles of cross-breeding the nigger and the horse as we stated above, the purpose of which is to create a diversified division of labor thereby creating different levels of labor and different values of illusions at each connecting level of labor, the results of which is the severance of the points of the original beginnings for each sphere illusion.

Since we feel that the subject matter may get more complicated as we proceed in laying down our economic plan concerning the purpose, reasons, and effect of crossbreeding horses and niggers, we shall lay down the following definitional terms for future generations:

1.) Orbiting cycle means a thing turning in a given path.

2.) Axis means upon which or around which a body turns.

3.) Phenomenon means something beyond ordinary conception and inspires awe and wonder.

4.) Multiplicity means a great number.

5.) Sphere means a globe.

6.) Cross-breeding a horse means taking a horse and breeding it with an ass longheaded mule that is not reproductive nor productive by itself.

7.) Cross-breeding niggers means taking as many drops of good white blood and putting them into as many nigger women as possible, varying the drops by various tones that you want, and letting them breed with each other until the circle of colors appear as you desire. What this means is this: Put the niggers and the horse in the breeding pot, mix some asses and some good white blood and what do you get?

You got a multiplicity of colors of ass backward, unusual niggers, running, tied to backward ass longheaded mules, the one productive itself, the other sterile, *the one constant, the other dying—we keep the nigger constant for we may replace the mule for another tool, both mule and nigger tied to each other, neither knowing where the other came from neither productive for itself, nor without each other.*

Controlled Language

Cross-breeding completed, for further severance from their original beginning, *we must completely annihilate the mother tongue* to both the new nigger and the mule and institute a new language that involves the new life's work of both. You know language is a peculiar institution. It leads to the heart of a people. The more a foreigner knows about the language of another country the more he is able to move through levels of that society. Therefore, if the foreigner is an enemy of another country, to the extent that he knows the body of the language, to that extent is the country vulnerable to attack or invasion of a foreign culture. For example, you take a slave, if you teach him all about your language, he will know all of your secrets, and he is then no more slave, for you can't fool him any longer, and *being a fool is one of the basic ingredients of and incidents to the maintenance of the slavery system.*

For example, if you told a slave that he must perform in getting out *"our crops"* and he knows the language well, he would know that *"our crops"* didn't mean *"our"* crops, and the slavery system would break down, for he would relate on the basis of what *"our crops"* really meant. So you have to be careful in setting up the new language for the slave would soon be in your house, talking to you as *"man to man"* and that is death to our economic system. In addition, the definition of words or terms is only a minute part of the process. Values are created and transported by communication through the body of language. A total society has many interconnected value systems. All these values in the society have bridges of language to connect them for orderly working in the society, but for these language bridges, these many value systems would sharply clash and cause internal strife or civil war, the degree of the conflict being determined by the magnitude of issues or relative opposing strength in whatever form. For example, if you put a slave in a hog pen and train him to live there and incorporate in him to value it as a way of life completely, the biggest problem you would have out of him is that he would worry you about provisions to keep the hog pen clean, or partially clean, or he might not worry you at all. On the other hand, if you put this same slave in the same hog pen and make a slip and incorporate something in his language whereby he comes to value a horse more than he does his hog pen, you got a problem. He will soon be in your house.

Did Willie Lynch Succeed in Creating the Ideal Slave?

Now that you have read the WLL you should be in a better position to recognize and understand the effects of slavery and severe oppression. With this understanding, African Americans can begin to implement a reversal of the psychological slave programming they have been subjected to. It will be essential for all African Americans to begin to correct their thought process if they are to become independent and self-sufficient. African Americans must also understand that they are not powerless as a people. Throughout history, African Americans have accomplished much, have endured much, and have contributed much to America. African Americans have survived over and over again against the seemingly insurmountable obstacles that have been placed in their path.

Yes, Willie Lynch did succeed in his efforts to create a slave out of the African. Willie Lynch predicted that if his methods were used properly, the African would not only become a good slave but would become self-perpetuating for several hundred years, teaching their offspring to be good and compliant slaves and to accept oppression as a way of life. In effect, African Americans have been brainwashed and psychologically programmed to accept white society's standards and definitions and to reject that which is uniquely African or black. Essentially, many African Americans struggle in vain to be what they cannot be—white. Michael Jackson, who literally re-created himself in the image of whites, represents the most extreme example of having the "slave mentality," or what I more accurately describe as a particular kind of personality disorder that I call "oppression personality disorder-I." How sad it is when one cannot accept himself or herself as beautiful, intelligent, and worthy as a person. Many African Americans go to extreme and sometimes ridiculous lengths to transform themselves as a way of conforming to the white image. One example is black-skinned women and men dying their hair blond and wearing blue contact lenses; these people will typically respond by stating that it is just fashion. Other examples include skin-bleaching cream, hair perms, changing one's natural vocal tone in order to sound white, and so on. Many African Americans are so deficient in their self-concept that many of them seek to be recognized and endorsed by whites before they will be able to feel a sense of self-worth.

This phenomenon is similar to the abused-child syndrome. African Americans to a large extent are like the abused child who has suffered at the hands of her caregiver. (I use a female example here, but of course the child could just as well be male.) The abused child endures the maltreatment with the hope that if she conforms to the expectations of her abuser, she can or will be treated with love and consideration. The abused child is confused psychologically, because she cannot understand what she has done wrong to deserve the abuse she has suffered. Since the abused child has not behaved in a way that warrants such punishment and abuse, she eventually begins to blame herself as being innately bad. Therefore, she continues to seek the love and acceptance of her abuser, even if that person is her caregiver. In this regard, there is a convoluted relationship between the child/African American and the caregiver/slave master. African Americans cannot understand why whites treat them the way they do, especially since the two groups have such a long and intertwined history.

African Americans thus believe that if they prove themselves worthy, the whites will love and appreciate them. As a result, many African Americans work very hard to please their white coworkers, bosses, and other whites whom they come into contact with. Some of them try so hard to gain the favor of whites that they become self-sacrificing; they also become willing to deface other African Americans when they feel that to do so will secure their acceptance and acknowledgment by whites. This strange collateral relationship has been noted throughout history both during and subsequent to slavery. It is quite interesting, for example, how the black person in the movies is nearly always killed or dies, while the white people survive. In many of these movies, it appears that African-American characters willingly sacrifice themselves for the survival of their beloved white associates. If you have traveled lately by air or visited a federal building, you may have noticed that African Americans are often on the front line, protecting the welfare of society. Whites know that African Americans can be trusted to protect them, even if it means that they will have to sacrifice their own lives. To this end, African Americans tend to value recognition and approval from whites, to the extent that they completely devalue their own identity and well-being in deference to another culture that, by and large, has oppressed and continues to oppress them. This behavior is counter to normal and healthy psychological functioning.

A normal and healthy personality is developed from positive affirmation from one's own cultural environment (community and family). Because the affirmation that African Americans seek from whites will never be realized, African Americans are thus caught in a quagmire of mental-health dysfunction and self-destruction. Movement toward emotional healing and healthy mental functioning can only be achieved through African Americans' development of positive self-recognition and self-affirmation. African Americans have to develop a healthy and positive self-regard and a positive regard for other African Americans. At the core of dysfunctionality among African Americans is the concept of self. African Americans have attempted to define themselves based on the standards of white society and culture; they have accepted white standards for evaluating themselves and for evaluating one another. The self-concept is how a person views and sees him- or herself. Since African Americans are naturally different from whites, they are automatically unable to meet the standards set by white society. Yet African Americans attempt in vain to emulate and imitate whites in many respects. The evidence supports Willie Lynch's prediction that his methods of creating a slave of the African would continue well into the future.

The remainder of this book is an effort to assist African Americans in their journey to attaining psychological health and freedom, which can only be achieved through knowledge and an understanding of the conditions that have misdirected them from knowing their true selves.

Chapter II: The Impact of Slavery and Oppression

The Psychological Impact of Slavery

American slavery and oppression of the African was the most unusual occurrence in the history of humankind. K. M. Stampp describes the inhumane treatment of African Americans in his 1956 book *The Peculiar Institution: Slavery in the Ante-Bellum South.* Many authors have written about and described the experience of slavery. By all accounts slavery and the exploitation and the mistreatment of African Americans have all been described as horrific. In order for slavery to be justified in the minds of whites, African Americans had to be designated as subhuman. Once African Americans were designated and accepted to be subhuman, then and only then could whites avoid the fundamental principles of morality and the laws of God when dealing with the African. Therefore, questions of morality and moral principles were not applicable to the African or other people of color. In fact, it was this dehumanizing of the African by whites that provided the justification for the subjugation of all nonwhite people throughout the world. Only white people were considered where questions of morality were concerned. Because the African was deemed subhuman, the consideration and protection afforded to whites under the principles of moral law did not apply to the African. Since Africans were deemed subhuman, whites treated them in a strict commercial frame of reference. This subhuman view of the African amounted to a collective conscious denial by whites of the innate humanity of the African.

This view of the African as subhuman amounted to a perversion of moral reality to suit the greed of a few. It must be understood that the vast majority of whites agreed with (or at least passively agreed with) the idea and the practice of slavery. Some whites did object to the practice of slavery, and some whites sought to assist the African in achieving freedom from slavery. The vast majority of whites chose to adhere to the social order of the time, however, thus creating a social institution based on slavery that has stood for over 465 years. Even after slavery was abolished, African Americans were still not free. For the next hundred years, African Americans were forced to live under oppressive laws known as the

Jim Crow laws. African Americans were not afforded the right to life, liberty, and the pursuit of happiness that white Americans were afforded. As a result, African Americans had to endure another hundred years of legalized and systemic oppression until 1964 and the passing of the Civil Rights Act (CRA), culminating in 1965 with the passing of the Voting Rights Act (VRA). It is not surprising that African Americans continue to suffer from the harsh and unusual punishment inflicted by slavery and systemic oppression.

It bothers me immensely when I hear presidents and other politicians talk about "human rights" violations by other countries and nations. The human rights of African Americans were and continue to be denied. African Americans have to keep reminding themselves of the oppression they have endured in order to remain vigilant. Because of slavery and legal oppression, African Americans have developed dysfunctional behaviors that continue to cause them much pain and suffering. The negative psychological effects of slavery and oppression continue to linger; the lasting effect is present in the psychological and behavioral functioning of African Americans today. The behavior of African Americans has received much attention and has been a popular topic for many years for various sociologists, psychologists, psychiatrists, social workers, counselors, and others. Although much has been published on the dysfunctional behavior of African Americans, all of these efforts have fallen short of being able to provide a diagnostic label that would explain the dysfunctional behaviors of African Americans. Without a doubt, slavery and oppression have had their effects on the psychological development of African Americans. It should not come as a surprise that African Americans continue to exhibit many dysfunctional behaviors as a result of slavery and oppression. The key issue lies in understanding "how" African Americans were psychologically programmed and how that programming evolved into the dysfunctional behaviors that stem from slavery and prolonged oppression. Certain methods had to be implemented in order to make a slave. The WLL represented this effort at implementing methods to create a slave out of another human being. In order to accomplish this goal, the African was subjected to dehumanizing psychological programming that was reinforced with punishment and a threat to life.

The WLL stated that "the black slave after receiving this indoctrination shall carry on and will become self-refueling and self-generating for three hundred years, maybe thousands." Having established this indoctrination, Lynch gave a warning. He made this warning to say that if the psychological programming of the slave was not properly reinforced and nurtured, there was the possibility the psychological programming could fail. In this sense, his warning stated,

> Our experts warned us about the possibility…for they say the mind has a strong drive to correct and recorrect itself over a period of time. If it can touch substantial original historical base; and they advise us that the best way to deal with this phenomenon is to shave off the brute's mental history and create a multiplicity of phenomena of illusions.

The challenge for African Americans today is thus to "correct and recorrect" their minds from the damage inflicted upon them by hundreds of years of slavery and oppression. In order to do this, an intimate understanding of African and African-American history is an essential part of the solution. We will discuss the role of history at more length in later chapters.

Slavery and oppression have laid the foundation for the disorder that I have designated OPD-I, which permeates every single aspect of African-American life on a daily basis. Regardless of income, education, age, or gender, our practice has found OPD-I to be present in the thoughts and behaviors of all African Americans to some degree at some point in their lives. No matter their socioeconomic level, OPD-I tends to be present and operating. I have not met any African Americans of slave descent in whom OPD-I was not present to some extent. No doubt some people will disagree with my thesis. Those African Americans who would still disagree with me after reading this material are probably in denial, however, and may be suffering from an illusion, as outlined in the WLL. If African Americans are to continue moving forward in their quest for complete freedom and independence, then they must address and correct the 465 years of psychological programming that has occurred and is still in effect today. Before personal and collective goals and aspirations can be fully realized, African Americans will have to recognize the ways in which they have become dehumanized, self-destructive, and dysfunctional.

The Post-1965 Disconnect

For years I have been baffled about why African Americans have failed to thrive as well as they should. Before 1964–65, African Americans were able to develop a significant infrastructure within the African-American community. For the most part, African Americans were self-sufficient prior to 1964 in spite of the Jim Crow laws. They possessed practically all the requirements for self-sustaining communities. They owned their own community stores, funeral homes, schools and colleges, banks, and other institutions and businesses. The African-American community was, for the most part, quite self-sufficient, although African Americans did not have any rights under the law. Prior to the passage of the CRA of 1964, African Americans were forced to remain in their own communities and to work together for the common good. After the passage of the CRA of 1964, African Americans began to pursue a misguided agenda of integration. As of this writing it has been fifty years, and integration has not yet occurred in the sense that African Americans envisioned. When will African Americans realize that whites do not intend to include them in their world? Their purpose is to maintain power and control over all others, especially over African Americans. Africans Americans must accept this fact and the fact that whites have no intention of sharing anything with African Americans. If they do, it is only to the extent that it will improve their position and purpose of control.

One major problem that the African-American community faces is the lack of a common agenda. Instead of having a common agenda, what African Americans have is a situation in which everyone is working from a narrow personal agenda. Of course, it is difficult to establish a common agenda if a common purpose is not first established. Once African Americans understand their individual purpose as African Americans, they can begin to formulate a common agenda to be addressed and implemented. The efforts of current African-American leaders are fragmented and disjointed. For example, what is the primary goal and agenda of the African-American church? What is the agenda of the National Association for the Advancement of Colored People (NAACP) today? What is the agenda of People United to Save Humanity (PUSH)? What is the agenda of the Southern Christian Leadership Conference (SCLC) today? What is the agenda of the National Association of Black Social Workers (NABSW)? What is the agenda of the Association of Black Psychologists (ABPsi)? What is the agenda of the National Council of Negro Women (NCNW)? What is the agenda of the various college fraternities and sororities? What is the agenda of the Black Political Caucus (BPC)?

I am not saying that these organizations do not address important issues. It appears that the efforts of these organizations are fragmented, however, and that there is a tendency to focus on narrow issues that often fail to be generalized to the greater African-American community. I believe African Americans must begin to focus on the problems that exist within the African-American community: issues that African Americans can have a direct impact on, such as truancy, high-school dropout, teen pregnancy, drug abuse, HIV/AIDS, STDs, lack of economic development, and so forth. Unfortunately, African Americans have been programmed to focus on their differences rather than their commonalties. In "The Making of a Slave," Willie Lynch stated that "I have outlined a number of differences among the slaves, and I take these differences and make them bigger. I use fear, distrust, and envy for control purposes." As a result, one can witness this slave programming and OPD-I at work within African-American organizations today. Remember that Willie Lynch's primary tactic was to highlight and magnify differences as a way of keeping African Americans divided and in conflict with one another.

African Americans must establish a common agenda for all of their organizations if they want to be more effective in dealing with the issues that face the African-American community. Too often, any significant agenda that an African-American organization has inevitably takes second place to egos and personal agendas. African-American leaders thus have to rise beyond their own narrow personal agendas. African Americans are currently similar to the adolescent. The adolescent has entered maturity but still lacks the ability and knowledge to be economically self-sufficient; so it is with African Americans. African Americans have gained their personal freedom under the law but still lack the ability to be economically self-sufficient as a community. Although African Americans have money and economic resources, there is no collective consciousness about creating an economic power base. Many African Americans do not understand that money represents power and that without money they are powerless. They tend to view money as a means of consumption at the personal level; as a result, African Americans continue to be economically dependent on whites and continue to endure oppression. African Americans have the financial means at their disposal to become economically self-sufficient, but they remain economically dependent and socially oppressed because they do not have a collective economic agenda.

THE YARD DOG

In order to exemplify what I mean by African Americans disconnecting from their community, let us consider the following example of the "yard dog." Some African Americans remind me of a yard dog who has spent his entire life behind a fence or on a chain. This yard dog has no conception of freedom or any experience of being free. Consequently, when the yard dog is set free, he will roam without purpose and will never return home again—either by choice or because he does not know the way home. African Americans are like the yard dog in that they do not know or understand the requirements of freedom. They seek to escape their own communities, believing that what they seek is elsewhere; they do not realize that they cannot fit in where they are not wanted or not welcomed. We can see this all over the country: African Americans who flee their own communities to invade (excuse me, integrate) white communities, only to have the whites move and leave the blacks behind in what ultimately becomes another African-American community. African Americans must realize that they have to begin to build their own communities and that there is no escape to another world. African Americans have been so oppressed and deprived that they do not understand or appreciate their own value or the value of one another. Nor do they take pride in what they do have. Too often,

African Americans will fail to embellish what they inherited from their parents and grandparents.

Many simply abandon property left to them by their parents and grandparents because of their misguided aspirations to live in the white world and to divorce themselves from their own communities. African Americans still suffer the negative psychological programming of slavery that has resulted in the condition of OPD-I. As a result of this personality disorder, African Americans tend to disassociate themselves from one another. While attending a baccalaureate at a predominately white church, for example, I saw another African-American man with his family. Our eyes met and I spoke to him, but he did not respond; he just looked at me as if I were an alien or an "invisible man," as described by Ralph Ellison in his book *Invisible Man*.

I have experienced this kind of behavior many times, where African Americans will not acknowledge one another when they are in a majority-white environment. African Americans have learned— excuse me again, they have been taught—to not acknowledge or openly recognize one another, because to do so implies rebellion against white control. To me this lack of acknowledgment at church was yet another example of OPD-I and the effects of slavery and oppression at work. Perhaps African Americans are afraid that by acknowledging one another they are sending a message of solidarity with other African Americans and that they share a common bond in their history of struggle for freedom and dignity. Whatever this man's reason was for not speaking to me, I was left feeling sad and frustrated at his inability, in reality, to acknowledge himself— because I was a reflection of him.

Chapter III: Understanding the Effects of Slavery and Oppression

OPD-I and the "Mark of Oppression"

Kardiner and Ovesey describe the dysfunction of African Americans in the title of their aforementioned 1951 book, *The Mark of Oppression*; OPD-I is the "mark of oppression" that Kardiner and Ovesey referred to. The devastating effects of slavery and oppression have been understood and recognized for a long time by those in the behavioral health-care field. Until now there has not been a name or a clinical diagnostic label that would describe and encapsulate the overall effects of slavery and oppression on the psychological development and functioning of African Americans and others who have experienced prolonged systemic oppression. OPD-I represents a highly dysfunctional personality disorder that involves a way of thinking and behaving that is peculiar to African Americans (as well as to other nonwhite individuals who share a racial and cultural history that is similar to what African Americans have experienced).

OPD-I is perhaps the most frequently occurring disorder and is the single most devastating mental-health condition experienced by African Americans today. OPD-I is the result of prolonged oppression experienced by African Americans stemming from over four hundred years of slavery and another one hundred years of legal, social, and economic oppression. Encounters where African Americans experience attitudes of racism and discrimination serve to reinforce and amplify OPD-I among them. Like other personality disorders, OPD-I is a psychological defense mechanism. OPD-I represents the primary defense mechanism that African Americans use to cope with the psychoemotional pain and distress caused by prolonged oppression. The primary source of dysfunction among African Americans today can be traced to the manifestation of OPD-I. Regardless of the Axis I diagnosis (see definition below)—whether it be adjustment disorder, substance abuse disorder/substance dependence disorder, anxiety disorders, mood disorders, depression disorders, suicide, or other mental-health disorders—the OPD-I, an Axis II diagnosis, represents a primary source of dysfunctional behavior among African Americans. (The American Psychiatric Association's *Diagnostic and Statistical Manual of Mental Health Disorders*, or *DSM*, uses five "axes" or categories to record and document mental-health disorders; Axis I is used to record all mental-health disorders except for personality disorders, which are recorded in Axis II.)

Marriage and family issues, parent-child issues, and other personal and interpersonal problems represent, in part, the influence of OPD-I among African Americans. It is necessary for African Americans to first understand the nature of their psychological dysfunction in order to devise a remedy and a solution for restoring the African American to healthy psychological functioning. Many African Americans in the behavioral health-care field have long recognized the dysfunctional behaviors that African Americans exhibit. OPD-I is in part characterized or expressed by the black person's attempt to become white or white-like in his or her thoughts and behaviors. In Frantz Fanon's 1952 book *Black Skins, White Masks*, the author states that "the ultimate goal of the black person is to become white or to become as close to white as possible." Because black people have accepted "the white standard" to define themselves by, they have placed themselves in a no-win, losing proposition, because the black person can never achieve "whiteness."

Yet African Americans struggle in vain to achieve "whiteness" in practically all they do. If you examine African Americans' motivations, you will see the quest and the desire to be white. Nathan Hare describes in his 1965 book *Black Anglo-Saxons* the various attempts that African Americans have made to conform to white society. By and large, African Americans and other oppressed people of color around the world experience the same conflict within their beings. African Americans, in particular, have accepted the psychological programming that being white is desirable and that being black is undesirable or even a curse. African Americans thus try in vain to become white or at least white-like. African Americans are like children who imitate their parents. They have accepted white values, beliefs, and behaviors as the standard by which they must judge themselves and to which they must aspire to in order to become acceptable as human beings. Instead of worshiping God, African Americans are worshiping white people; indeed, many African Americans believe Jesus was white. A survey that our practice conducted to assess African Americans' beliefs (see the appendix) revealed that approximately 30 percent of respondents believed that Jesus was white. African Americans' belief that Jesus was white serves to further reinforce dysfunctional views of the self.

Consider how ridiculous it is to define oneself in terms of another—especially one who is the opposite of you. How insane is this? It's like a man who aspires to be a woman or a woman who aspires to be a man. We know of people who have these sexual-identity disturbances. No matter what they do, they can never become the opposite sex. These people can act and dress as the opposite sex and even undergo surgery to alter themselves physically, but ultimately they cannot achieve their goals. In the end, what you have is a very distorted and confused individual who is neither fully male nor fully female (as the case may be). The same is true for racial identity; people can never change who and what they are. Yet African Americans have attempted to betray themselves in order to become something that they cannot be: white. One symptom of OPD-I is thus manifested in the attempt to become white. White society will never fully accept a black person as an equal no matter his or her economic status, educational status, complexion, and so forth. This is why so many African Americans who are high achievers become frustrated: they can never fully gain acceptance by whites because of the color of their skin. In the white world, everything is defined on the basis of skin color. The sad fact is that African Americans have also permitted skin color to influence and define various aspects of their lives. African Americans' emphasis on skin color is a manifestation of OPD-I. Remember that Willie Lynch used skin color as one of the methods of dividing the slaves on the plantation.

OPD-I and the Need for a New Diagnostic Category

Sociologists, psychologists, psychiatrists, social workers, counselors, and others have devoted considerable attention to African Americans' behavior and have developed numerous theories over the years to explain the phenomenon. A plethora of books, research articles, journal publications, and the like have sought to examine and explain the unique behavioral aspects of the African American. A partial list (please see the references section for more) would include DuBois 1944; Clark and Clark 1939, 1950; Clark 1965; Kardiner and Ovesey 1951; Jahoda 1958; Karon 1958; Popper 1963; Fanon 1963, 1967; Moynihan 1965; Grier and Cobbs 1968; Kardiner and Ovesey 1951, 1968; Mosby 1972, 1980; Thomas and Sillen 1972; Guterman 1972; Gynther 1972; Wilcox 1973; Edwards 1974; Lazarus 1975; Wright 1975; Tyler 1978; Griffin and Korchin 1980; Williams 1981; Houston 1984; Cross 1985; Akbar 1990, 1991; Nobles 1991; J. M. Jones 1991; A. C. Jones 1991; Leary 2005; Parker 2008; and Kambon and Bowen-Reid 2009. While these writers have attempted to analyze the nature and circumstances that define the psyche of African Americans as descendants of an oppressed history in America, they have been unsuccessful in providing a diagnostic label that would encapsulate the unique African-American experience as it relates to psychosocial development. For example, Doris Y. Mosby published an article in 1972 in which she discussed the need for a unique theory of personality for African Americans. She advocated the advancement of a theory of personality that would encompass the unique aspects involved in the formation of the "black," or African-American, personality. The lack of a definitive clinical diagnostic category has made it impossible to accurately diagnose or treat the core issues that confront African Americans.

As many theoreticians have noted in the past, the use of Eurocentric conceptualizations, theories, models, and diagnostic categories will not work effectively for African Americans in the healing process (Clark and Clark 1939, 1950, 1965; Grier and Cobbs 1968; Mosby 1972; Cross 1979, 1985, 1991). An appropriate diagnosis is necessary before we can expect to effectively treat African Americans and other oppressed peoples. An appropriate diagnosis that would take into account the unique aspects of the African-American experience is not included in the existing classification system of mental-health disorders. Therefore, it is both necessary and appropriate that the existing classification of personality disorders be expanded to include a category that would take into consideration the unique psychosocial issues that are experienced primarily by African Americans. An appropriate diagnosis is required before African Americans can expect to achieve healthy psychological functioning.

It is customary in clinical practice to operate on the premise of a theoretical framework that explains the conditions and nature of the issues that clients experience. This theoretical modeling or framework is structured and established as the perspective that is used to explain the issue or problem that is being investigated or treated. Once the theoretical framework is established, the issues or questions are framed for testing and validation in the field based upon appropriate research designs. After much testing, the results yield findings that are then accepted as verification of the theoretical model, which in turn guides the development of various treatment approaches. To date, the state of science in terms of definitive research and interventions and a theoretical framework for mental-health issues that African Americans face remains unfinished and inconclusive.

It is this specific void in the field that I have sought to address in my work. Past works on the subject—for example, DuBois 1903; Kardiner and Ovesy 1951; Karon 1958; Grier and Cobbs 1969; Blauner 1972; Mosby 1972, 1980; Clark and Clark 1939, 1950; Cross et al. 1991; Akbar 1990; Ramseur 1991; Robinson 2000; and Leary 2005—have all approached this issue and have described the various psychological dimensions that have been influenced by oppression. These authors and other social scientists have also discussed the frailties and the dilemmas of the African-American personality by comparing the African-American psyche to that of the Anglo-American psyche (Jahoda 1958; Mosby 1972). These works have failed to acknowledge that there is no definitive description that would delineate what exactly would constitute a state of "healthy mental functioning" for African Americans or what the determinants would be for a healthy personality for African Americans. One of the most fundamental barriers to African Americans being able to achieve a healthy psychological state of functioning is the fact that African Americans are trying to define their identity from a societal context that is counterproductive to the attainment of their well-being. Mosby (1972) wrote that "the black person grows up on the margin of a white dominant culture, which makes him feel inferior." She further states,

> The personality of the black person is molded, determined, shaped by a dominant and generally

aversive cultural influence. As a result of continuous repressive restrictions and inferiority perceptions, he internalizes inadequacy, achieves at best a precarious mental balance, and develops into a fragile human being. This cultural influence appears to counteract and override the potentially positive factors of his innate influences and of his own subculture.

Perhaps a recap of the introduction in the 1972 reissue of William Grier and Price Cobbs's seminal work *Black Rage* (1968) captures the essence embodied in this work. The authors conclude in their introduction that *"the most important aspect of therapy with blacks is that racist mistreatment must be echoed and underlined as a fact: an unfortunate fact, but a most important fact. Dissatisfaction with such mistreatment is to be expected, and one's resentment should be of appropriate dimensions. It bears some resemblance to military psychiatry, where the psychiatrist must keep fit for duty the warrior whose primary function is to oppose the enemy. In America, the role of blacks, as for humans everywhere, is to live and flourish and to be fit progenitors of generations to come. To do so, they must oppose racism in an unrelenting way. Psychiatry for such warriors aims to keep them fit for the duty at hand and healthy enough to enjoy the victories that are certain to come."*

It is from this orientation that I have constructed a new paradigm as a theoretical perspective and framework that will provide a backdrop and a context for understanding the psyche and mental health of African Americans. As per Mosby's suggestion in 1972, OPD-I now provides for a "theory of personality that encompasses the unique aspects involved in the formation of the African American personality."

DIAGNOSTIC CRITERIA FOR OPD-I

The diagnostic criteria established for OPD-I are based on results from clinical research, clinical case reviews, client feedback, and relevant literature. The premises established for the criteria were based on African Americans' responses to the list of criteria outlined in the following section. If three or more of the following criteria are present, oppression personality disorder is indicated. The *DSM-V* (the fifth edition of the manual, updated in 2013) describes a personality disorder as:

> ...an enduring pattern of inner experience and behavior that deviates from the expectations of the individual's culture and is manifested in at least two of the following areas: cognition, affectivity, interpersonal functioning, or impulse control (Criterion A). This enduring pattern is inflexible and pervasive across a broad range of personal and social situations (Criterion B) and leads to clinically significant distress or impairment in social, occupational, or other important areas of functioning (Criterion C). The pattern is stable and is of long duration, and its onset can be traced back at least to adolescence or early adulthood (Criterion D). The pattern is not better accounted for as a manifestation or consequence of another mental disorder (Criterion E) and is not due to the direct physiological effects of a substance or general medical condition (Criterion F).

The *DSM-IV* (originally published in 1952) further states that "The diagnosis of a personality disorder requires an evaluation of the individual's long-term patterns of functioning, and the particular personality features must be evident."

The *DSM*-type criteria for OPD-I include African Americans who

1. want and feel a need to be validated by white people and white society;

2. emulate the behavior and characteristics of white society (exhibit and express a preference for the white value system or desire to be white);

3.   seek to minimize distinguishing African characteristics (e.g., hair, eyes, nose, skin color, exaggerated and altered speech tone, and general self-rejection);

4.   tend to oppress and punish rather than accommodate other African Americans (generally expressed by a disassociation with other African Americans and a tendency toward minimizing and/or undermining and sabotaging the efforts of other African Americans);

5.   lack significant knowledge of and identification with African-American history (generally unaware or have sparse information about African-American history);

6.   exhibit self-destructive tendencies (alcohol and other drug use, sex, gambling, prison recidivism, etc., as a result of self-hatred);

7.   exhibit antisocial behaviors (generally expressed with violations of the law and multiple incarcerations, especially in violations of the rights of other African Americans, such as physical abuse, homicide, assault, and other acts of violence);

8.   show personal identity disturbance (depersonalization, detachment, derealization, apathy, and/or experiences of anxiety and/or depression);

9.   are unable to articulate a specific sense of purpose as African Americans (vague and ambiguous, lack specificity);

10. overly rely on religion and/or God (i.e., the otherworldly) as a source of equity and justice (religious addiction, passivity and apathy, a "wait on the Lord" and "turn the other cheek" attitude, fear of having to assume personal responsibility for one's circumstances, personal responsibility relinquished to God vis-à-vis a pastor);

11.   exhibit generalized learned helplessness and a generalized sense of fear (view race as a personal liability, have a sense of personal helplessness, or powerlessness; are overly dependent on others; seek to relinquish responsibility; detach or withdraw from social and civic responsibility; fear reprisal by white people; lack assertiveness when confronted by white people);

12.   have an external "locus of control" (i.e., a tendency to seek external validation from whites);

13.   exhibit generalized anger and aggression (hostility, the presence of an elevated anger baseline, inappropriate expressions of anger, rejection of social norms, antisocial behaviors);

14.   use compartmentalization as the primary psychological defense mechanism.

These criteria serve as a basis for understanding the fundamental sources of psychoemotion dysfunction that inhibit a sense of self-affirmation and a continued sense of group dissociation. Clinical studies have validated that OPD-I is present and operating for African-American clients in treatment.

Having established the presence of OPD-I as an overarching basis for behavior, my use of this perspective to treat clients has been able to effectively address many of the presenting problems of my African-American clients. I am hopeful that other professionals who provide behavioral health-care services to African Americans will help establish OPD-I as a viable diagnostic category that will be included in the next version of the *DSM*. The American Psychiatric Association (APA) would make a giant step forward in improving the quality of treatment for African Americans by adopting and including OPD-I as a viable diagnostic category to be included in the *DSM*. If the APA is unwilling to recognize and accept the validity of OPD-I, however, then African-American therapists and organizations (such as the Association of Black Psychologists, the National Association of Black Social Workers, and the Association for Multicultural Counseling and Development) will have to take the lead in forging a new path for the effective treatment of African Americans and similarly oppressed cultural groups. African Americans can no longer afford to wait to be affirmed and validated by the majority culture before moving forward with adopting more effective and appropriate treatment approaches.

Now that a name and a context have been given to the complex set of experiences that adversely affect African Americans, the professional therapeutic community (as well as individuals) now have a new clinical tool and a new conceptual framework to guide their work with African-American clients in their approach to mental-health treatment.

MEASURING OPD-I

Once I understood that African Americans suffer from OPD-I, the next question became: What is it that African Americans think and believe as a collective? We refer again to the WLL, where Lynch states, "They advise us to shave off the brute's mental history and create a multiplicity of phenomena of illusions." In an effort to understand the beliefs and thoughts of African Americans, our practice developed a questionnaire to obtain the perspectives and the beliefs that African Americans hold. We developed and used the Psychosocial Development Scale for African Americans (PDSAA) to gather responses from a cross section of one thousand African Americans. The original questionnaire consisted of sixty-two true or false questions (see the appendix). Many of the findings of the PDSAA questionnaire were surprising and yet enlightening. The PDSAA also represented an effort to identify and quantify the presence of OPD-I among African Americans. Some of the responses to the PDSAA will be included in discussions of the healthy African-American mind below.

THE PSYCHOLOGICALLY UNHEALTHY AFRICAN AMERICAN

Frantz Fanon discussed and analyzed the effects of colonialism (slavery and oppression) on the psyche of blacks in two books: *The Wretched of the Earth* and *Black Skins, White Masks*. Kardiner and

Ovesey, in their book *The Mark of Oppression*, also discussed the devastating impact of oppression on the lives of African Americans; *Black Rage* (Grier and Cobbs 1968) is another seminal book on the black psyche. These writings represent efforts to describe and comprehend the effects of oppression in the lives of African Americans; these authors have been accompanied by many more who have sought to understand and explain the psychological perils experienced by African Americans. The following list represents some of the characteristics of the oppressed and unhealthy African-American mind. The oppressed and unhealthy African-American mind exhibits several traits:

- denial; avoidance of responsibility toward African-American history
- poor concept of self; rejection of self; lack of positive self-regard
- self-defeating behaviors: work inhibition, incarceration, drugs, etc.
- learned helplessness: the making of excuses rather than assuming personal responsibility; reliance on welfare
- envy and hatred of other African Americans; preference for whites and white society
- devaluation of self and others of like kind; black-on-black crime; lack of collective identity
- victim mentality; blaming of personal failure on whites
- economic mismanagement (personal and public); abandonment of African-American infrastructure
- willingness to compromise other African Americans for personal gain and the support of oppressors and oppressive agendas
- desire (or need) to be accepted and acknowledged by whites as a primary motive for behavior
- general disrespect for black authority and leadership
- tendency to disrespect and minimize other African Americans

We may generally identify these characteristics (which are all indicators of OPD-I) as typical manifestations of various cognitive distortions that have been created by prolonged oppression.

As noted elsewhere, OPD-I is present and operates in virtually all aspects of African-American life on a daily basis. Some selected areas of African-American life that manifest the behaviors associated with OPD-I will be described and examined below. In addition to examining the dysfunctional behaviors that define OPD-I, we will also discuss a strategy for developing healthy psychological functioning in later sections.

OPD-I and Motherhood Dysfunctions

According to Willie Lynch, in his discussion on "The Breaking Process of the African Woman":

> If you break the female mother, she will break the offspring in its early years of development and, when the offspring is old enough to work, she will deliver it up to you, for her normal female protective tendencies will have been lost in the original breaking process...in her natural uncivilized state she would have a strong dependency on the uncivilized nigger male, and she would have a limited protective tendency toward her independent male offspring and would raise the female offspring to be dependent like her. Nature has provided this kind of balance.

According to this logic, the goal of slave making was therefore to reverse this natural balance between male and female roles by altering the basic tendency of the African female and mother. The following excerpt from "The Making of a Slave" section describes the process:

> We reversed nature by burning and pulling one civilized nigger apart and bull whipping the other to the point of death...all in her presence. By her being

left alone, unprotected, with the male image destroyed, the ordeal caused her to move from her psychological dependent state to a frozen independent state. In this frozen psychological state of independence she will raise her male and female offspring in reversed roles. For fear of the young male's life she will psychologically train him to be mentally weak and dependent but physically strong. Because she has become psychologically independent, she will train her female offspring to be psychologically independent. What have you got? You've got the nigger woman out front and the man behind and scared. This is a perfect solution for sound sleep and economics.

It is a sad fact that the psychological conditioning process of the African-American female as proposed by Willie Lynch has worked out all too well, as witnessed today in how African-American mothers raise their sons and daughters. A saying in the African-American community is as follows: "We raise our daughters, and we love our sons." We may still observe this tendency today in the twenty-first century. The tendency of African-American mothers to indulge and enable their sons in becoming dysfunctional is exemplified by the irresponsibility and dependency of many African-American males. Many African-American mothers are unconsciously committing "emotional incest," as Love and Robinson (1990) put it. One can also witness the "handing over" or delivering of their sons up to the system. This delivery takes the form of juvenile delinquency, school dropout, low academic achievement, and countercultural activity (poor work orientation and work habits, drug use, drug selling, and other conduct disorders). I have witnessed on numerous occasions African-American mothers hand their sons over to the juvenile-justice system because of their dysfunctional parenting as a result of OPD-I.

One profile of African-American mothers includes the mothers who become mothers at an early age—during their teenage years, well before they are prepared to take care of themselves, much less a child. Most often these teen mothers were themselves the product of teen mothers. As a consequence, the necessary parenting skill to raise healthy children is not present. Even more so, mature African-American mothers tend to undermine their male children by being overly indulgent and creating dependency and fostering irresponsibility.

Related to this dysfunctional mothering behavior is the practice of some African-American mothers to figuratively "eat" or destroy their children by abdicating their parental role of caring for and nurturing their children into responsible young adults. At a very extreme level, some African-American mothers who engage in drug use set their sons and daughters to prostituting and selling drugs to satiate their own drug habits. Being in this broken, drugged state leaves the mothers irresponsible and without moral authority; their children most often become victims of physical, emotional, and even sexual abuse. These traumatic experiences lead many youth to engage in drug use and other self-destructive behaviors. In far too many cases, these abused children gradually end up self-destructing and become involved in the criminal-justice system after committing various violations of the law. While juvenile departments adhere stringently to their law-enforcement and compliance requirements, they pay little heed to adequately assessing the psychosocial and emotional circumstances of children or youth to ensure appropriate treatment. Getting to the root of the problem is the last priority of the "system," which is driven by economic dictates. Breaking this cycle of delinquent behavior will require comprehensive psychosocial assessments and referral to appropriate treatment and support services for both the juvenile and his or her family. "Acting-out" behavior is most often symptomatic of problems in the family. Juvenile departments most often direct their attention to the children, because they are powerless victims of adult failures.

AD/HD SYNDROME

Once African-American boys enter the educational system in America, the problems begin to surface (Kunjufu 1985). African-American boys who display any degree of assertiveness or offer the slightest hint of opposition or defiance are quickly labeled a problem or difficult children. Anything less than complete submission and compliance is deemed to be problematic. In my clinical practice, I have encountered a large number of mothers who have presented their young sons for behavioral counseling on the recommendation of a teacher or school official. Even before we can complete an assessment, these mothers tell us that a teacher or principal has labeled their young sons as having attention deficit disorder/hyperactivity disorder (ADD/HD) and that their sons need to be medicated in order to control their behavior in the classroom and at home. Many of these mothers became mothers in their teens—unmarried, poor, and fairly uneducated—and have put their faith in the school personnel. Surprisingly, these mothers have already accepted that their sons have a problem, especially if they have experienced any acting-out behavior at home. Many middle- and upper-income mothers also tend to place their confidence in the school system and psychiatrists and accept their diagnosis of their sons. As a consequence, many African-American mothers are unquestioningly ready to comply with school systems in medicating their sons in order to control their behavior. African-American mothers have unknowingly become collaborators in the Lynch-style "breaking" of their male children by enabling irresponsible behavior, by being overly protective, by being domineering and intrusive, by being emotionally detached, or by being emotionally enmeshed. If these mothers experience acting-out behavior by their sons, too often they will look to the juvenile-justice system to relieve them of their responsibility as a mother and as a parent. These women essentially relinquish their sons to the "system" because the mothers have implemented the dysfunctional system of mothering described by Willie Lynch.

CASE EXAMPLE OF "MARK"

"Mark" was a sixteen-year-old African-American male who was referred to our facility for substance-abuse treatment and to participate in our therapeutic after-school program. After a few weeks we discovered that Mark's mother had given birth to him when she was sixteen. Mark's mother had two other younger children, ages six and four. Mark's mother was never married, and each child had a different father. Mark's mother was feeling overwhelmed by her responsibility to take care of her children; she was unemployed and received welfare. She was very involved in her church and was going to school full time. She was required by the juvenile court to attend parenting classes and to participate in counseling with Mark. When staff approached Mark's mother to arrange for counseling sessions, her response was that she didn't need counseling; it was Mark who had the problem and not her. She stated that she had a life, that Mark was messing up her life, that Mark's behavior was not her fault, and that she would not attend any kind of counseling. She also stated that he would just have to be locked up, because she was not going to inconvenience herself and neglect her activities and her life because of him. A few weeks later, Mark ran away from home and was subsequently locked up in the local juvenile facility for an undetermined amount of time. In all likelihood, Mark will remain in the juvenile-justice system until he turns eighteen.

As this case example illustrates, Mark's mother had developed an emotional detachment from her own son and was also living in denial of her responsibility to Mark and her own lack of maturity. As a result, she was more than willing to have Mark out of her home and in the custody of the juvenile authorities. In effect, she was behaving in the manner that Willie Lynch predicted. She handed over her son to the system and was totally unaware of how she had sabotaged her own son's life by her own irresponsible behavior, which was another instance of OPD-I. Unfortunately, this pattern of behavior is fairly common among those African-American families where the mother (generally single) became pregnant as a teen and had limited education and support systems.

At the other extreme are the African-American mothers who are overly indulgent and overly protective (in particular of their sons). These mothers are often in conflict with the father in terms of parenting and discipline style. Some middle-class mothers seek to limit the disciplinary efforts of the father, especially where the male child is concerned. I have spoken to numerous couples who were in conflict over parenting practices and disciplinary issues; a male child is involved the majority of the time. These mothers seek to protect their sons from the harshness and sternness of the father. Often these mothers are guilty of undermining the parental authority of the father, and often with an open display of defiance toward the father's attempts to disciple the son. In some instances the mother will even create a secret alliance with the children against their father. This overly protective attitude by some African-American mothers is another manifestation of OPD-I.

Although these issues are generally not associated with the parenting of daughters, I have witnessed mothers who were jealous of their daughters' relationships with their fathers. Typically, African-American mothers rarely come into conflict with fathers about the disciplining of their daughters. Many fathers have a different attitude and a different approach when interacting with their daughters than with their sons. African-American mothers generally teach their daughters to be responsible and self-reliant.

OPD-I and Fatherhood Dysfunctions

Many African-American men fail at being responsible fathers. A major reason for this failure is because too many African-American males did not have a father in their own lives. Based on statistics provided by the National Foundation for Fatherhood, approximately two-thirds of African-American youth are currently being raised without the presence or involvement of their father. As a result, many African-American males have no idea of what it means to be a father, since they did not experience having a father in their own lives. Many African-American males have thus abandoned their responsibilities as fathers or have a distorted notion about how to fulfill their roles as fathers. This fatherhood dysfunction is another manifestation of OPD-I.

It is my belief that this tendency of African-American men to abandon their responsibilities as fathers can be linked to slavery and oppression. During slavery, African-American men were used as studs to breed more slaves; they were not permitted to act as fathers and husbands. Families were separated. Children were separated from their fathers, mothers were separated from their children, and women were separated from their mates. Children were permitted to live with their mothers from early childhood to adolescence, however, in order for the mothers to train their children in the ways to accommodate oppression and slavery. The slave owners relied on the mothers to reinforce and carry out the breaking process. This breaking was focused especially on male children. Seldom were slaves permitted to live as intact families. As a result of separating families, African Americans had to endure a unique psychological pain. In order to cope with this emotional and psychological pain, it is plausible that African-American men and women had to emotionally disengage themselves from their offspring and from one another. This was especially true for African-American males, as they were prevented from bonding with their offspring. The bond between children and their father was most affected.

I believe that slavery is responsible for some African-American men's emotional disengagement, abandonment, and general irresponsibility toward their children today. It is undeniable that slavery has had a profound impact on the trend of irresponsibility by African-American men toward their mates and their children, just as described in the WLL. Even when slavery ended, due to the existence of Jim Crow laws, African-American men were unable to provide for their families as they could have. African-American men and their families had to endure another hundred years of legalized oppression by the American government. African-American men in particular were systematically oppressed and kept out of the economic mainstream: more so than African-American women. Remember Willie Lynch's treatment of the African woman. She was made a co-conspirator in the effort to control the African male. African-American women have and are granted greater freedom and mobility within white society, thus placing the African-American male as the second and less powerful figure. Several generations of African-American men were therefore forced to assume marginal roles within the family. It has been extremely difficult for African-American men to assume the role and responsibility of fatherhood as defined by the majority culture. The impact of this situation can still be witnessed today.

These hardships are not an excuse for African-American men not assuming their roles as fathers; rather, it is a reality of the African-American experience that needs to be understood and corrected. The cycle has to be broken. African-American men have to understand the tremendous power and influence they have in the lives of their children. It is my belief and observation that children define themselves by their father rather than their mother. The father determines a child's identity and sense of self as a person. We have discovered through our work with children and adolescents that many of the problems they experience is a direct result of the father's absence. Children and adolescents who lack fathers in their lives tend to have more significant emotional and behavioral problems. The most common symptom of father absence is anger and defiance toward authority. When these youth are asked to discuss their relationships with their fathers, they express a range of generally negative responses. Among the responses that I have heard include *I hate that nigger, I don't know my father, I will beat him if I ever meet him, I don't like my father, I don't care about him*, and so on.

Most responses about relationships with fathers tend to be emotionally negative in tone. These boys are likely to grow up and repeat the same kind of irresponsibility toward fatherhood as their fathers have. Growing up without fathers has left emotional wounds for many men, and as a result of this emotional devastation many men are unable to develop the kind of empathy to assume responsibility for their own children. When my son was young, for instance, I involved him in a number of sports. I would always volunteer to assist with the teams. While working with my son's teammates it became very apparent to me, while observing the behaviors of these boys, which of them had fathers and which did not have fathers or other significant males in their lives. The boys who did not have fathers in their lives tended to be less aggressive and more insecure, they tended to give up sooner and complain more, they tended not to follow instructions as well, they displayed a greater lack of self-confidence, they missed practice more, and they tended to drop out or quit more. I observed that the boys who did have fathers in their lives displayed greater self-confidence and persistence, followed instructions better, complained less, and were more aggressive.

When a child has a father in his life (and again, this could refer to girls as well as boys), he will interact with the world with greater confidence because he has some "backup"—his father. Children are less fearful and feel more secure in general because they have their fathers to protect them. Without the presence of a father, children generally tend to become more fearful, because they do not have a backup and they feel unprotected. Children without fathers are therefore less assertive and tend to be more fearful and hesitant when it's time to interact with the world. Only fathers can provide the kind of emotional security that children need in order to develop into healthy and competent adults. I am not saying that mothers do not provide emotional security for children, but I am saying that the kind and type of emotional security provided by mothers is different. Mothers cannot provide the same sense of security and protection that fathers can; women rely on men to provide them with emotional safety and protection, just as children do. African-American men have to fully understand and appreciate their importance in the lives of their children and their families.

Too many African-American men have abandoned their responsibilities as fathers and do not understand and appreciate the importance of their role as fathers. As a result of abandonment by African-American fathers, there is a general tendency toward what I refer to as *father hatred* in the African-American community. I believe father hatred contributes to the difficulty that African-American men have in working together. Think about it: If you have a general hatred and disrespect for your father, the most important and the most significant male in your life, then how can you have respect for any other man? I believe this father hatred is responsible for the high rate of "black-on-black" homicides and other black-on-black crimes. Dr. Alvin Poussaint, a professor of psychiatry, addressed this issue in his 1972 book *Why Blacks Kill Blacks*.

My sense of purpose was conveyed to me by my father, my grandfathers, and other significant males in my life. The purpose for my life was communicated to me both verbally and by example. Beginning at an early age, I was taught the nature of my existence and the purpose for my existence. Today, as I have matured and experienced life, I have come to understand and recognize that many African-American males do not understand their purpose in life. It has become clear to me that many African-American men suffer from a lack of purpose and direction in life. I have observed too many African-American males struggling in vain for personal fulfillment. Over the last twenty-five years of conducting therapeutic interviews with African-American male clients, it has become obvious to me that much of the conflict and dysfunction that African-American males experience is directly related to their lack of understanding of their purpose as men and as fathers. Many of the African-American males I have seen as clients have been incarcerated for various violations of the law, and many have also been caught in the trap of substance abuse and addiction. As a part of my therapeutic approach with these men, I uniformly ask them about their purpose in life. At first this was simply my way of getting them to take an objective look at themselves and their life. Almost without exception, these men would tell me that they had not thought about this question before. Many would also say to me that this was a good question, that they were wondering the same thing, and that they wished that they did know their purpose in life.

Most of these African-American males were forced to seek therapeutic counseling as a condition of their probation or parole. Considering the demographic profile of this group of men, it is to be expected that they would not have identified any worthwhile purpose for their lives. The obvious assumption is that if they did have a worthwhile purpose for their life, then they would not be in the desperate situation in which they found themselves. The profile for these men generally includes early dropout from school (generally about the tenth grade); early encounters with the legal system, beginning in adolescence; early experimentation with alcohol and other drugs; no significant male role models; a childhood in which they were raised by single mothers; reliance on public assistance as the primary source of financial support; the experience of emotional, physical, and sexual abuse, or some combination of these, as well as experience with other emotionally damaging experiences. Most if not all of these men would be classified as having mental and behavioral disorders. No one would expect these men to have a clearly defined purpose in life beyond mere day-to-day survival.

As I expanded my study, I discovered that African-American males from the best of homes, with both parents present in the household, college educated, blue- and white-collar employment, and middle- and upper-level income, struggled with the same lack of definition in their lives. This group of African-American males defined themselves in terms of their occupational and economic status. When pressed to respond to the question of what purpose their lives served, most responded that their purpose was to be the best person they could possibly be or to be the best person at their chosen occupation and to be successful. Many others responded that their purpose in life was to help others and to set a good example. Another common response by this group of African-American males about their purpose in life was to fulfill God's plan and to serve God.

When asked about God's plan for them, however, these men still did not have a clearly defined response.

The majority of African-American males with whom I have discussed what I believe to be their purpose in life have embraced and recognized the validity of my view of their purpose. African Americans will state their individual goals, but they cannot articulate their purpose in life as an African American. The common purpose of all African Americans, from both yesterday and today, is the ongoing struggle for life, freedom, and liberty and the fight against oppression. Those African-American males who have identified with and have accepted this common purpose have reported a positive change in their lives and a renewed feeling of pride and a sense hope for their lives. It is the embracing of this common purpose for African Americans that has brought about a restoration for the African-American males I have worked with in my counseling practice. Many of these men have begun to assume their responsibilities as fathers and as husbands once they have understood their purpose. Systemic oppression has caused many African-American men to devalue both themselves and one another. The system has used and continues to use many ploys to undermine and devalue the African-American male. A present-day example is "affirmative action," in which African-American females are worth two EEOC (Equal Employment Opportunity Commission) points while employment of an African-American male is worth only one EEOC point.

Another ploy is the current welfare policies that support the single female head-of-household family structure. This arrangement mirrors what Willie Lynch described in his methods for making a slave: remove the male from the home, thus making the female psychologically and emotionally independent and without the influence of the male figure. Because of this, it is up to the African-American male to break the cycle of fatherhood abandonment by assuming the awesome responsibility of fatherhood. In order to correct and to break the cycle of fatherhood abandonment, it is necessary for African-American men to get in touch with their greatness as only knowledge of African-American history can provide. African-American men built America. They have served and fought in every war that threatened America, beginning with the American Revolution. African-American men served in the Civil

War, as Buffalo Soldiers, and in World War I, the Korean War, World War II, and the Vietnam War. Yet African-American men returned home to an America where they were not afforded equal rights under the law. African-American men have served and fought for America with distinction and with little or no acknowledgment or gratitude by the country they fought for; America continued to perpetuate negative images of black men and sought to devalue them.

African-American men have to embrace the truth about their existence, which can only be appreciated with a thorough knowledge of their own history in America. Willie Lynch stated that the "mind has a strong drive to correct and to recorrect itself" if one can acquire a knowledge of history. Of course, Lynch encouraged the slave owner and subsequent oppressors to hide the history of African Americans and their contributions from them. The regretful thing is that many African-American men do not appreciate the achievements and accomplishments of their ancestors and forefathers. This is why a thorough study of African-American history is a vital and necessary first step in the overall solution of correcting the psychological and emotional dysfunctions that all African Americans experience. Finally, African-American men have to understand that if they do what is right for their children, they will always make the right decisions and will experience pride.

OPD-I and Education

African Americans have placed their children in the hands of their enemy. It is ridiculous that African Americans could believe that others who are in direct competition with them would empower their children with the knowledge to compete with and defeat them in their agenda of exclusion and control. Yet African Americans continue to place confidence in their oppressors in preparing their own children to compete with their oppressors' children. This is why the public schools are still predominately black and brown. White people of any financial means at all place their children in private schools or move into areas where African Americans are not present or are present in very small numbers. The oppressors of African Americans do not intend to share the kind of knowledge and information that can benefit African Americans' children. I am reminded of Carter G. Woodson's 1933 book entitled *The Mis-Education of the Negro*. Many of the points he makes in his book and in his many other writings are still true today.

African-American boys in particular experience difficulty in public and private school systems across America. An acquaintance and colleague of mine, Dr. Twyla Williams, published a book in 2009 entitled *Save Our Children: The Struggle between Black Parents and Schools*. In her book she discusses some of the issues and attitudes of the white-controlled schools and their seemingly oppositional stance toward African-American children: especially toward African-American male children. Increased dropout rates and truancy are high for African-American youth, especially African-American male students. African Americans have to encourage and nurture a value for education within their children. Low-income African-American children tend to be the ones who need education the most. In our work we routinely ask African-American youth what they want to do when they grow up and finish high school. Almost without exception, the most frequent response from low-income African-American youth is that they want to be rappers or sports professionals in the NBA or the NFL. Yet these same youth do not consider that their best chances of becoming sports professionals will be by matriculating through college. When they are asked what they want to be or what they want to do if they do not become rappers or sports professionals, they most often state that they do not know. The other plan for success we often hear is that they can make money by selling drugs and hustling. The sad part is that some African-American parents actually encourage and support their children in these misconceived aspirations.

The introduction of crack cocaine to the African-American community has served to further undermine the moral values of many within that community. During the late 1970s and throughout the 1980s, adults began to use children to sell drugs because Children and juveniles would not face the same penalties under the law as adults. Misguided adults therefore began to involve and exploit children as drug dealers. Today I encounter young adults who represent the second generation of drug dealers. This practice still occurs today by ignorant and misguided African-American adults: instead of encouraging their children to value education and legitimate work, many African Americans have succumbed to the lowest common denominator of corrupting their children for their own greater financial gain. African Americans must restore the value of work, education, and learning.

The typical low-income African-American family that we work with in our facility has an average of three televisions, one of which is a rented "big screen." They have stereos, cable, the latest video games, all kinds of CDs and DVDs, and the latest smartphones for their children, but books and artwork are nowhere to be found in these homes. These same low-income African-American families dress their children in the latest Nikes, Tommy, FUBU, Sean John, Polo, and so forth, but these same parents have not saved a dime for their children's education. They have all the trappings to suggest or portray that they are living the American Dream. They believe that to have these things means they are equal to and as good as others in America. These adults emphasize appearance rather than substance to their children. Their existence is purely superficial: they are attempting to buy or rent a lifestyle that reflects what they believe to be the American Dream. It is unfortunate that these poor, uneducated, and misguided African Americans believe they are living in the mainstream. When the youth of these African-American families are asked to name the title of the last book they have read, they cannot name a title or an author—but they can name the last CD or DVD they bought. When we do home visits with some of these youth we can barely hold a conversation over the multiple televisions and the stereo. There is little encouragement to read or to study. In fact, many African-American youth feel that if they are studious they will be viewed as nerds. Many African-American youth hide their intelligence and ability because they do not want to be criticized by their peers. Their African-American ancestors have worked long and suffered much to access education only to have their descendants abandon these educational opportunities. I often remind African-American youth that there was a time when African Americans were not permitted to read and were severely punished for attempting to do so.

The most destructive influences in the lives of African-American children and youth are the television and radio, and now the Internet. Many African American households have more than one television. Many African Americans spend several hours per week being programmed by the voices and images presented on television. Children as well as adults are being programmed with negative and destructive images. If you turn on the television on any given evening you will find two to four hours of African-American sitcoms portraying African Americans as jokers, fools, and clowns. There is very little in the television media that portrays African Americans as serious, intelligent, and accomplished people. The other images African-American youth are bombarded with are the themes of sex, violence, and materialism celebrated in rap music and videos. For the first time in history, ignorance, banality, and mediocrity are rewarded and represented as something to aspire to. In short, "ghetto" has gone mainstream.

It is African-American youth who are primarily influenced by these negative and amoral images. These images promote irresponsibility, which leads to substance abuse, school dropout, violence, crime, and premature sexual activity (which then results in teen pregnancy and HIV/AIDS). While these children could look up to a number of positive African-American role models and responsible and successful African Americans among us today, these positive images of success and responsibility remain in the shadows. This is why African-American parents must return to teaching the basic values of education and honest work that will ensure the success of their youth. African-American history has to be valued and taught at home, since very little African-American history is taught in schools or referenced in the textbooks that are used in the public education system. African Americans must turn off the television, the stereo, and the video games and encourage more reading and thinking. The average African-American child spends an estimated 26,280 hours—that's 3,285 days or 469 weeks—watching television by the time he or she reaches eighteen years of age. The youth we work with tell us they spend about three hours per evening on the phone with their friends. Between the television and the phone, African-American youth are spending approximately one-half of their waking hours on nonproductive activity. The other 50 percent of their time is spent acting out what they have seen on television. This acting out includes using drugs, having sex, and fighting. With this constant bombardment by the media, it is not surprising that too many African-American youth are misguided in their perception of life.

African-American parents must become involved in the education of their youth. Our agency works with the truancy courts. Without exaggeration, thousands of youth find themselves in the truancy courts every year. It is not the fault of the teachers or the school district. In practically every case, the parents of these children are not involved in the education of their children. The majority of these parents have never attended a PTA meeting; nor do they know the names of their children's teachers. We witness the tendency of noninvolvement by the parents of these children. The truancy courts refer these children to our facility for assessment, counseling, and community service. Unless we insist that the parent (or parents) meet with us, they will drop them off. Some have commented to me that it is not their problem; they did not know why they had to participate. As mentioned earlier in the case of Mark, one mother commented that her son was "messing up her life" and that she had a life and was not responsible for his behavior; they could "lock him up" for all she cared. This represents the kind of attitude we often encounter by too many African-American parents. Typically, these parents were high-school dropouts and teen mothers and fathers. We are witnessing a cycle of intergenerational teen parents. We encounter cases where African-American girls are having babies beginning at age fourteen—their mothers and their mothers' mothers all having been teen parents—and the cycle continues. We currently work with at least three generations of teen parents. How can uneducated children effectively raise children? When a teenage girl becomes pregnant, her education is most often permanently disrupted (or at best delayed). Education is also part of the overall solution to correct the lingering effects of slavery and oppression.

CASE EXAMPLE OF "JAMES"

I was acquainted with a youth whom I will refer to as "James." James was referred to our agency when he was sixteen years of age for truancy and possession of marijuana. James lived with his mother and five-year-old younger sister. James's father was thirty-five and lived in the city with his mother. James spent little time with his father; this was probably a good thing, since James's father was an alcoholic and worked only sporadically, doing construction work. James did not present any real problems for the staff or me. In fact, he appeared to enjoy his time at the facility. He was cooperative and never oppositional. It was a difficult and ongoing task, however, to help James relinquish his dysfunctional family programming. He did not have a strong value for work, and he was not motivated to continue his education. James eventually violated the terms of his probation and was sent to the state youth commission until he turned eighteen. When he turned eighteen and was released from the youth commission he came to visit with me and to obtain my help and advice. James stated that he was doing odd jobs and was saving up to buy a Cadillac. I advised James not to buy a Cadillac but to buy a used pickup truck and a used lawnmower and some yard equipment so that he could earn a living. I explained that another young man I knew had done the same thing and had eventually established a very lucrative lawn-care business.

About a month later, James came to see me and to show off his newly acquired 1978 Cadillac El Dorado. He was very proud of his acquisition. He stated that he was now saving up for some chrome wheels and a new stereo system. The very next day, James called me because he was stranded nearby and could not get his car to start; he didn't know anything about maintaining a car. I went to where he was stranded. His battery was dead and he needed a new one, but he didn't have the forty dollars required. He asked me to loan him some money, and I denied his request. James was a little angry with me for not loaning him the money, but I told him that a new battery would not change his situation. He looked at me with puzzlement. James was able to get money somewhere for a new battery. About a week later, I saw James at a fast-food restaurant. I asked him how things were going with his car; he told me that the car now needed a starter that would cost about $450 for parts and labor because it was a front-wheel drive. About a year later I saw James's mother, who told me he was now in prison for drug possession with intent to sell.

This case example of James is a typical scenario for too many young African-American males. James first of all failed to acquire an education and did not value honest work; he wanted immediate gratification, as is the case with so many African-

American youth of today. Throughout my life, starting as a young child, the need for an education has been continually reinforced by everyone in my community. Today, however, the message to secure a good education can barely be heard. Instead, the messages that young African Americans hear emphasize sports, entertainment, and even dope dealing as the means to obtain success. Some misguided youth believe that going to prison is a prerequisite for success, as some rap artists have experienced. In other words, they are attracted by what appears to be the shortcut or the easy road, and they seek instant gratification. African-American parents have to discipline their children early and teach them to become persistent in their efforts regarding work and valueing education and learning. They must be taught that delayed gratification is necessary in order to achieve their goals and that obtaining an education and a skill is absolutely necessary for any measure of success in life. The great Booker T. Washington offered a solution for success to African Americans in his 1901 book *Up from Slavery*. His solution for achieving success and leading a productive life was very simple: the African American should "get an education and learn a skill, buy land and save money." This formula is still viable today; education is as important today as it ever was if African Americans are to overcome the effects of oppression.

OPD-I and Religion

Just as many African Americans suffer from drug addiction, many suffer from what various authors refer to as "religious addiction" (Booth 1991; Arterburn and Felton, 1991; Vanderheyden 1999). It appears, from my experiences and my interactions with African Americans, that many have given up on this life and are waiting to die, believing that death will provide them with a better existence than the one they currently have. The vast majority of African Americans practice Christianity in some form (i.e., Baptist, Methodist, African Methodist Episcopal, Church of Christ, Holiness, Jehovah's Witnesses, Catholic, and Presbyterian, among others). Unfortunately, Oppression Personality Disorder-I as it is expressed in the religious orientation of African Americans (especially within

Christianity) is especially damaging and represents perhaps the greatest area of dysfunctional behavior among African Americans. The present situation that is occurring in the African-American church has not always been the case. In the last forty years or so, however, the focus and agenda of the African-American church has undergone a drastic deviation from its history of practicing a "theology of liberation," as James Cone put it in his 1986 book *A Black Theology of Liberation.*

In the past, the African-American church practiced a theology of liberation. The African-American church was intimately involved in the fight for freedom and for civil rights for African Americans since the beginning of slavery. The African-American church was central to the progress that African Americans have gained over the past two hundred years. In the past, the African-American church served as the staging ground for social and political action. From Harriett Tubman and the underground railroad to Martin Luther King Jr. and the civil rights movement, the African-American church has been at the forefront in African Americans' ongoing quest for freedom and equality. The African-American church of today appears to have lost its vision and purpose. It appears that African-American preachers and pastors have lost their connection to the ongoing struggle for freedom and equality in America. I was talking with a pastor recently about what he believed to be the purpose of the African-American church today and the role the church played in the struggle for African-American freedom. He responded by stating that he believed that discussing slavery all the time was not good and that people (referring to African Americans) were tired of talking about slavery. This pastor expressed the sentiment of many African Americans. It is unfortunate that when the topic of African-American history is brought up, many African Americans think only about slavery—as if slavery were the sum total of African-American history. African-American history is so much more than just slavery. Because many African Americans are ignorant of their own great history, however, they view African-American history in a very narrow context; they do not realize nor appreciate the many outstanding accomplishments of African Americans.

I grew up in a Baptist church and have supported various churches throughout most of my life. Today, however, I believe that

African-American churches are failing to address the current needs of their congregations. African Americans still have a lot of work to do in order to gain their fair share of the American Dream. The next phase of the African-American struggle is to acquire the economic power that has long been denied them. But African Americans will have to change their strategies if they hope to address the next phase of their long-standing quest for freedom and justice. Now that African Americans have freedom under the law, they now have to learn new ways to move forward. African Americans have to redefine their goals as a people and devise new strategies to achieve these new goals. I believe that African Americans have had the same goal from the beginning as they still have today: to pursue the same life, liberty, and happiness that America has supported for its white citizens. Without collective economic power, however, it is impossible to achieve these goals. African Americans have been denied freedom for over 465 years now; the job of the African-American church is not finished. In fact, the most difficult battle still lies ahead. The African-American church must learn and embrace a more relevant theology. Many pertinent models exist for an activist church. For example, *Holy Change: A Systematic Approach to Transforming a Community* (2008) by Dr. Joseph Parker Jr. has outlined a model for the church to seize its biblical charge to reclaim "the city" in the biblical sense. African Americans have to become an economic and political power in America, just as Jewish Americans have become. Once economic power is established, African Americans can realize political power. Many may argue that African Americans already have economic and political power, but they are wrong: I am not simply speaking about the ability to spend money, as African Americans are currently doing. I am referring to African Americans' goal of establishing their own banks and other financial institutions. I am not speaking of just simply being able to vote. Rather, I am speaking about the kind of political power that only money can afford. I am speaking of having the political wherewithal to influence legislation through economics rather than social protest alone.

The African-American church represents the primary collective economic power in the African-American community. Just as in the past, the African-American church will have to lead the way. Thus it will be the responsibility of the African-American church to stimulate the acquisition of economic power within the African-American community. I am not speaking about nonprofit community development corporations (CDCs). CDCs do not empower the African-American community economically, because nonprofit organizations by their very nature cannot empower anyone. Many CDCs have proliferated over the past twenty years as a slick and not particularly deceptive way for the white-owned banking industry to address the mandate of the Community Reinvestment Act of 1984, which was to assist African-American entrepreneurs and businesses in accessing capital. The sad truth is that African Americans accepted this compromise because our political and religious leaders sold out or were ignorant of the economic implications of the legislation. The majority of CDCs are established and implemented by church-affiliated organizations and other community-based nonprofit organizations. In the end, the African-American community is not economically empowered by CDCs. African-American businesses and African-American entrepreneurs still don't have equal access to capital, and as a result there is little to no business development or business activity in the African-American community. Yet African Americans attend "megachurches" that deposit millions of dollars into white-owned banks weekly.

In practically every African-American community in America, you can observe other people of various cultures and races operating businesses within the African-American community. Just about every convenience store, nail salon, gas station, restaurant, dry cleaner, tire shop, liquor store, and yes, even funeral home, is operated by people other than African Americans. Maybe I am unique in my assessment, but to me something is very wrong with this situation. Now here is the real rub: every week, every Monday morning, the African-American community deposits from $50 million to $500 million in banks across America. Once this money is deposited, African Americans never see this money again. Where is all this money going? The money is being deposited into white-owned banks, and African Americans do not have access to their own capital when they want to do business. Young whites can get loans to establish all kinds of business ventures, while African-American young people have to take the low road and remain employees of whites and others whom African-American money have placed in business. In Dallas, Texas, where I live, there are currently five multimillion-dollar church facilities all located within a three-mile radius. Yet within this three-mile radius, African Americans do not have the semblance of any business equivalent to justify the existence of these megachurch facilities. In other words, while these megachurches are surrounded by businesses, few if any of them are owned by African Americans. In Dallas, African Americans don't have or own any banks or other financial institutions; the whole country, in fact, has a severe lack of African American–owned banks. The question is: Why don't African Americans own more banks? African Americans certainly have the money to establish their own banks and financial institutions. Maybe it is because African-American leaders, especially religious leaders, don't have the vision or will to do so. Perhaps it is too easy for them to just continue talking and selling hope. After all, talking is easier than taking action. African-American religious leaders have established their kingdoms on earth and cannot (or will not) address the larger issues the African-American community faces, such as AIDS, unemployment, drug abuse, violence, incarceration, school dropout, teen pregnancy, economic discrimination, and lack of care for the elderly. Even with former first president Bush's faith-based initiatives, African-American churches still fall far short of addressing these issues that their communities face.

Let's go back to the millions of dollars that African Americans deposit in the banks each Monday. These deposits amount to well over one billion dollars per year. Imagine what could happen if African-American churches formulated an economic plan and began working together and pooling their money. If the three or four largest churches in Dallas were to unite and put their money together, an economically strong bank could be established overnight. The African-American community would surely be blessed and truly liberated if this were to occur: no more waiting to die in order to experience the fullness that life has to offer today. The question is, why haven't our religious leaders sought to engage in real and significant economic development? Could it be the slave mentality at work? Could it be that out religious leaders cannot work together? Could it be that our religious leaders lack vision? Could it be that our religious leaders don't have the will? Could it be that they are simply content with things the way they are: with them on top and dictating to the rest of us? Could it be selfishness and greed? What is it?

I have come to recognize that like too many African Americans in general, too many African-American preachers and pastors do not know their history nor the role of the African-American church in the struggle for freedom. No preacher I have interviewed has read the aforementioned *A Black Theology of Liberation* or *The Negro Church in America* by E. Franklin Frazier (1963) or C. Eric Lincoln's *The Black Church since Frazier* (1990). They have not read *Green Power* by A. G. Gaston (1968) or *Economic Empowerment through the Church* by Gregory J. Reed (1994). I am sure of one thing, and that is that the African-American community will not become economically self-sufficient until their churches and religious leaders begin to unite in this effort. The African-American church must reclaim its role as the central focal point in the ongoing struggle for the complete liberation of African Americans, and therefore the church must return to a theology of liberation.

The African-American community has more churches than any other community in America. If going to church and the number of churches in a community made a difference, then African Americans should have the best community in the country if not the whole world. In spite of the number of churches in the African-American community, the levels of violence and social ills in the African-American community surpass those of all other communities. Indeed, the number of churches in the African-American community actually appears to be correlated with crime, poverty, and violence. The apparent indifference and irrelevance of the church to the true needs of African-American people makes church and spirituality unreal in the minds and souls of African Americans. Therefore, they fail to see the pertinence of the church in their everyday lives. (On a side note, black Muslims emphasize self-sufficiency and economic empowerment in their practice of Islam; whether you like them or not, the Nation of Islam appears to be on the right track in terms of working together as a collective and working together toward attaining economic independence and self-sufficiency. African-American Christians must begin to follow the example set by Jewish Americans and the Nation of Islam and begin to work toward economic self-sufficiency.)

Back to the topic of money, examples do exist of what is possible if African-American churches learn to work together. After all, African Americans for the most part believe and accept Jesus, do they not? Well, since the majority of African Americans accept and believe in Jesus Christ, it should be easy for African-American Christians to work together for the greater good of their community. Numerous people have in fact already set examples for African Americans to follow. In Birmingham, Alabama, for example, an extremely long-lived African-American gentleman by the name of A. G. Gaston (1892–1996) demonstrated the power of collective action on the part of the churches and the African-American community by establishing one of the strongest African-American banks in the country, Citizens Federal Savings Bank, in 1957. In 2004, Citizens Federal Savings Bank of Alabama merged with Citizens Federal Savings Bank based in Atlanta, Georgia. Gaston had been able to persuade the church and community to join together to establish a bank, and the bank received its charter in January 1957. As a result of his visionary undertaking to secure the financial destiny of his fellow African Americans, he was able to convince the churches to band together. The net effect of this effort was that the African-American community of Birmingham prospered as a result of church involvement. Dr. Gaston's involvement of the church remains a viable example of what is possible when the church comes together and embraces a common vision and a collective effort.

The African-American church has undeniably occupied the primary focal point for most, if not all, of the social and economic progress that African Americans have gained from the early beginnings. The African-American church has played a crucial role in the struggle for justice and equality; it has served as the catalyst for practically every significant movement within the African-American community. Historically, the African-American church has been central in the social and cultural lives of African Americans. The African-American church represents the most unified collective within the African-American community. It is within the African-American church that the seeds of progress have been planted and nourished. It therefore will most likely be the African-American church that will lead the way in the next episode of the African-American struggle—for economic self-sufficiency and economic power.

The next step in the ongoing revolution for African Americans is the achievement of economic self-sufficiency. After 465 years of struggle, it is now time for African Americans to secure their fair share of America. It was African Americans who played a vital and important role in helping America become the great nation it is today. Yet African Americans as a whole have not realized nor obtained their fair share of the American pie. In the past, as noted earlier, the African-American church assumed a central role in the progress that African Americans have attained. It will be (or should be) the African-American church that will lead the way to economic fulfillment and self-sufficiency, but first a few changes must occur within the church. The church leadership must adopt an agenda of economic empowerment and financial independence. The economic flow is presently one way: from the people to the preacher to the white banks and finance companies. This dynamic must shift to one where the economic wealth pooled from the people is channeled into instruments of institutional and personal financial well-being. The African-American church must lead the way in this next phase of the ongoing struggle for African Americans. The African-American church represents perhaps the only collective effort in the African-American community. Just think of the possibilities. If African-American churches begin to pool their financial resources and work together, African Americans could easily have their own financial institutions, such as banks, credit unions, insurance companies, finance companies, and so forth. There are no dollars for investment and job creation within the African-American community at present. What happens to all that money that African-American churches deposit each week? It is deposited into white-controlled banks and financial institutions. These same banks that refuse to embrace African-American business ventures use African Americans' money to further their own economic agenda of exclusion and economic oppression. The only thing African Americans have to show for their faithful giving to the church are larger and larger multimillion-dollar church buildings that stand idle most of the week. The monies that are collected by African-American churches seldom if ever find their way back to the African-American community. Even the huge churches that African Americans are so proud of are in reality owned by white financial institutions until they pay for them.

It is ironic that practically all Baptist churches in the African-American community have the term "Missionary" in their names. But who and what are the missions? For all the money that the church collects, it has established very few programs to assist in the development of their communities. African Americans are being duped—or, more harshly, they are being pimped—by their so-called religious leaders. This blind loyalty toward preachers and pastors is rooted in slavery and oppression and reflects one condition that defines OPD-I.

The white establishment historically allowed the African-American preacher certain privileges as a means of exercising further control over the masses of African Americans. This trend can be witnessed today. African-American preachers live comfortably while their congregations struggle and suffer. If you accept that African Americans have been engaged in a war for freedom, then you must also acknowledge that every war has its deserters, defectors, traitors, and collaborators. Too many African-American religious leaders today play the role of collaborator, either knowingly or unknowingly. I believe that many understand their role to be that of the collaborator and they choose to perform this role, just as during slavery times the black overseer often carried out his master's orders, often more cruelly than the slave master himself. The black slave overseer was especially cruel toward his fellow slaves in order to ensure his privileged position with the master. Like the black overseer of slave times, some African-American preachers today are permitted special privileges—as long as they help maintain the status quo. And the status quo is for African Americans to remain dependent and dysfunctional servants to an oppressive economic agenda.

In 1999 African Americans in Dallas, Texas were fortunate to have their first African-American police chief. The police chief was a good man by all measures. He was fair, intelligent, and capable of performing his role as police chief, and he did so for a few years until Dallas elected a female white mayor. Her desperate need to exercise her new power as mayor manifested in her firing the police chief for none other than racial and political reasons. This was an insult to the African-American community, which was demonstrably upset. Several religious leaders led a series of press conferences in which they vowed to unseat the mayor. The strategy was to have the mayor impeached by a recall election. In order for the recall of the mayor to take place, a petition requiring seventy-five thousand registered voters had to be collected and verified. The African-American preachers announced their strategy to the public and began to collect signatures. Months passed, but the preachers failed to accumulate the required number of names necessary for the recall of the mayor. Meanwhile, the mayor announced during news interviews that the ranting of these preachers did not at all worry or concern her.

You see, in Dallas, the white folks have learned to disregard the African-American community because that community has rarely followed through on any of the issues it has raised. The white leadership knew that they could count on the collaboration of the religious leadership, just as they had always done in the past whenever issues of race and discrimination were concerned. To make a long story short, the required number of signatures was never gathered, and nothing else has been said or done to address the African-American community's dissatisfaction over the capricious firing of the police chief. The issue just went away, as is the custom in this city when matters of justice and the African-American community arise. How difficult would it have been to collect seventy-five thousand signatures? If each of the five largest African-American churches in Dallas would have had their respective memberships sign the petition over a four-week period, then surely the required number of signatures could have been collected. Some African-American churches in Dallas have memberships in the thousands. The bottom line is that the African-American community was sold out once again by its religious leaders acting as collaborators in the quest for personal recognition and personal power. These religious leaders were essentially looking for endorsement from the white community: the stamp of acceptance and approval that so many African Americans seek in their need to validate themselves. This situation is just as described among the symptoms that define OPD-I.

Today in the African-American community one can witness the newest trends in church development. One can see huge, multimillion-dollar megachurches rising out of poor and modest African-American neighborhoods. Yet, as noted earlier, few business and commercial developments are undertaken in these same African-

American neighborhoods when compared to the proliferation of these new megachurches. The most successful and thriving business in the African-American community appears to be the establishment of a church. Indeed, some pastors whom I have spoken with talked in terms of the church being a business venture and a personal investment. Many times the church—both the building itself and the land it sits on—is actually owned by the pastor. The only new major form of construction that one may observe within the African-American community is the building of more churches or the conversion of properties to churches.

Religion is another kind of addiction for many African Americans, as Father Leo Booth refered to in his 1992 book *When God Becomes a Drug: Understanding Religious Addiction and Religious Abuse.* There is a difference between being religious and being spiritual. African-American religious practices amount to nothing more than a reinforcement of psychological oppression and the slave mentality. I have heard preachers say that black folk are like sheep and that they will follow without question anything their shepherds demands of them; this behavior can be witnessed today as African Americans stand by and support the slanderous and outrageous conduct of some of their pastors. African Americans no longer practice a theology of liberation as their forefathers and foremothers did. Instead, African Americans today practice a kind of escapism with an after-death focus.

It is good that more and more African Americans are becoming aware of the discrepancies that exist between what is said in the pulpit and what is being practiced on a daily basis. Enlightened African Americans are no longer willing to be sheep. Too many African-American preachers are "fleecing" the flock. Many of these preachers appear to suffer from an egocentric frame of reference and have narcissistic personality disorder. The message is clear: far too many African-American ministers feel the need to be in total control of every aspect of the church, including the lives of their members. To be fair, some African-American religious leaders attempt to address the issues within the African-American community. A very obvious example of this effort can be seen in the work of such progressive efforts as the Amachi Program, which has partnered with Big Brothers Big Sisters of America. The program, which was founded by the Rev. Wilson Good, former mayor of

Philadelphia, seeks to find, train, and match mentors from churches to work with children whose parents are incarcerated. The model is based on the belief that the African-American church is a strong institution that has the ability to garner a large base of resources to address the multitude of issues the African-American community faces. It also recognizes that a disproportionate number of African Americans make up the juvenile and adult probation and parole systems; thus, the African-American community through the church should play a major role in addressing the problems that these facts present. The program has met with some interesting challenges, however. While the success of the program in Philadelphia has led to a model that is currently attempting to replicate itself across America, program managers of the Amachi Program face barriers to effectively implementing the program. Responses from ministers have spanned the gamut from "I've been thinking about doing our own program" to "We don't want to get into that issue." If the ministers don't endorse the program, then the idea and the effort will die from lack of support. We thus see a mentality of "If I don't endorse it and can't control it, it's not going to happen."

Too many African-American religious leaders refuse to recognize their limited understanding, especially when it comes to social problem solving and business development. Their narcissistic personality permits them to believe that they are endowed with omniscience and that their knowledge and relationship with God is special beyond that of anyone else. The church membership is too docile and is overly willing to allow ministers to indulge their selfish interests and agendas above that of the community's welfare. Not only do the ministers tend to be egotistical, but they also refuse to recognize that within their church memberships a wealth of knowledge, expertise, and experience exists that can be harnessed to address the needs among the membership and among the community at large. Some ministers readily rebuke people who have attained PhDs or higher education, but they rush to take on the title of doctor or reverend doctor. If there is so much disdain for such titles, why do so many of them revel in the application of the title? They want it all. Ever since the Rev. Martin Luther King Jr. was awarded the Nobel Peace Prize and received an honorary doctoral degree, preachers have begun to take on this credential. Would Jesus want to be referred to as Dr. Jesus?

I also pose the question of why ministers so eagerly proclaim the call to the ministry yet fail to obtain necessary training to assume the role. Furthermore, why do so few ministers have full-time jobs in a chosen field in which they earn their livings doing what they are trained to do? Ministers are servants of God. Christ fulfilled his calling without pay. Today's ministers are not practicing the model that Christ set in the Bible. Some might argue that times have changed; while that is undoubtedly so, we should be reminded that Christ served outside the walls of a physical building. He also took his message and service to the people. The message is this: He did not need huge edifices to do God's work, he did not need titles to do his work, he did not need multiple mansions to do his work, he did not need $2,000 suits and unlimited wardrobes to do his work, and pastors need not have private jets, Rolls Royces, and the like to do his work. Too many ministers see the ministry as an easy way to amass personal wealth and gain social recognition.

All I am saying is that the African-American church appears to be operating from a very narrow orientation in terms of its mission as it pertains to the continued empowerment of the African-American community. I continue to witness in Dallas the proliferation of churches being built on an ongoing basis. Yet Dallas also has a historically black college called Paul Quinn College that is suffering. The college moved to Dallas in the early 1990s after the closure of another historically black college called Bishop College. While churches are continually being built, Paul Quinn College continues to struggle financially. And while some ministers and preachers drive Rolls Royces, Mercedes, Cadillacs, or Aston Martins, and some even have private jets, Paul Quinn College suffers financially. It is an indictment and a disgrace that a big city like Dallas, which has so many apparently wealthy black churches, would allow a black institution of higher learning to suffer. Paul Quinn College can do a tremendous amount to empower the African-American community by helping those who seek to become educated and to better their lives. While the churches are preparing their African-American congregations for death, Paul Quinn College is preparing its students for life. I don't know what else to say, other than that it is a shame that African-American churches and their leadership are so seemingly deficient when it comes to working for something other than their own self-aggrandizement. African

Americans are serving the church instead of the church serving them. Unfortunately, many African Americans who say they are Christians are too often devoid of any true spiritual understanding. It has become expedient to profess oneself a Christian as a device to cloak oneself while engaging in deviant spiritual behavior. The following case example is somewhat extreme, but it represents how Christianity and religion in general are too often used to cloak deviant behaviors, deviant agendas, and deviant acts under the guise of spirituality.

CASE EXAMPLE OF "MR. JONES"

One morning I received a call from a man whom I will refer to as "Mr. Jones." Mr. Jones wanted counseling for his grandson and his family. His insurance company had provided him with my name. He asked me several questions about my experience and my qualifications; mostly, he wanted to know if I was a Christian counselor. I informed him that I was a counselor who was also a Christian. He seemed to be satisfied with my religious orientation and scheduled an appointment. Mr. Jones and his wife arrived for their counseling appointment with their six-year-old grandson. After we spent some time establishing a rapport, Mr. Jones stated that they were seeking legal custody of their grandson, John, because the boy's mother was unfit to raise him. Mr. Jones explained that their daughter was a result of an interfamily adoption; in other words, their adopted daughter, Marie, was actually his wife's first cousin's child. They had adopted her when she was an infant, Mrs. Jones explained. Mr. and Mrs. Jones explained how Marie had begun to act out as she entered her teenage years. They discussed all the difficulties they had experienced with her while she was growing up in their home. They assured me that she had been provided with the best of care and that they had tried to give her the best life they could. Mrs. Jones stated that Marie had become pregnant with John when she was sixteen and that they had assumed the major responsibility for raising the boy. Marie had moved out of their home after she had graduated high school when she was eighteen.

Mr. and Mrs. Jones disapproved of her lifestyle. They stated that she used drugs and that she was involved in a lesbian relationship. They felt that her lifestyle was not a healthy one for John to be exposed to. Mr. Jones began to explain how the Bible considers a homosexual relationship to be a sin and that he would not have his grandson in this environment. The Joneses wanted me to conduct a fitness study to determine who would be the best parents for John. In short, they wanted me to side with them in their custody battle. I informed them that I would need several counseling sessions with John in order to determine his true feelings. I had learned from experience that there is always more to a case than what clients are willing to reveal. Mr. Jones stopped coming to counseling after the third session, believing he had laid the groundwork to establish the outcome for the counseling sessions. Mr. Jones believed that since I was Christian, I would side with him about his daughter's lesbian lifestyle and condemn her as he had done. He did not understand that as a professional counselor I do not impose my own values on others. So, fully confident, he had given the responsibility to his wife to bring John to counseling each week. During the sessions without Mr. Jones present, Mrs. Jones was able to provide additional information to me about their experiences with raising Marie. Mrs. Jones stated that their daughter hated her husband for no good reason; she explained how he was such a good and loving father to her and that he had accepted her as his own daughter. Mrs. Jones could not understand why Marie was so oppositional and defiant toward her and her husband. John appeared to be well adjusted to living with Mr. and Mrs. Jones since he had lived with them from birth. I explained to the Joneses that I also needed to interview their daughter. They assured me that she would not participate in counseling. Mr. Jones was adamant about their daughter's unfitness as a parent.

At this point I knew there was more to their story than what they were telling me. I had my suspicions. Daughters typically do not act out against their fathers without cause. I finally was able to talk to Marie on the telephone; I explained to her that I knew that there were two sides to every story and that I wanted her to help me clarify a few things about her son, John. She tentatively agreed to attend counseling. Although I never saw Marie in person, she did explain that her father was a liar and a hypocrite. To make a long story short, it turned out that Mr. Jones had been sexually molesting Marie since the age of twelve and that Mr. Jones was John's father.

This was the reason Marie was so angry toward Mr. and Mrs. Jones. She was angry because Mr. Jones sexually molested her; Mrs. Jones was in denial and had failed to protect her.

***

This example is just one of many where African Americans (and people in general) use religion to hide behind and mask their true character and deviancy. I have come to recognize that many African Americans use Christianity to justify and rationalize their behaviors. I have met very few African Americans who did not say that they believed in God. Yet few seem able to actualize their Christian beliefs in their daily affairs. In other words, there seems to be little to no congruence between what they claim they believe and what they practice in daily life. Religion has become a kind of escapism for many African Americans. They have chosen religious passivity instead of engaging in positive and productive resistance. African Americans expect God to make things right for them, while they remain idle. They assume no responsibility for transforming their lives once they accept Christ as their Lord and Savior. The essence of Christianity is that Jesus Christ paid for our sins, and upon our belief in him we are saved; this is the greatest event to occur in the history of humanity. The real question is, once you accept Christ, what do you do as a Christian in your daily life to manifest your beliefs?

Belief in Christ requires a transformation in the state of the mind (what we think) and heart (what we do). This change induces a state of peace, humility, generosity, and hope; a spirit of relatedness to all humanity; and ultimately a state of power over all earthly matters through Christ. The Christian is a positive-minded person who can rest in the power of Christ Jesus, who controls all things. The challenge as Christians is to unite in addressing the needs of their fellow men and women. The problems that humanity faces (poverty, addiction, ignorance, and disease, among many others) have been created by evil-minded people who choose to oppress and profit from these conditions and circumstances. As I discussed in my 2003 book *God's Prosperity*, God is a prosperous God who has provided all that is needed, but it is incumbent upon Christians to facilitate and ensure that the poor and needy receive assistance from the mountains of plenty. Each church and each member either addresses the worldly problems of their communities and congregations or they are a part of maintaining those problems. Unfortunately, the majority of African-American churches fail to embrace the needs of their communities. African-American churches, as a whole, are not engaged in a theology of liberation; they appear to be engaged in the exploitation and continued economic and psychological oppression of their own people. One manifestation of OPD-I is religious preoccupation to the point of complete submission of the will and a complete reliance on God to rescue them from the oppression they so willingly accommodate.

OPD-I and Marriage

The African-American male-female relationship has been severely damaged by the conditions imposed by slavery and legal oppression. Many African-American couples, married and unmarried, experience conflict and dysfunction within their relationships. Healthy African-American male-female relationships appear to be rare. Again, I know some will disagree with me and would assert that African-American marriages and relationships are no better or worse than those of other groups. I will be the first to agree that there is some very unique strength that African-American couples bring to their relationships. The fact remains, however, that many African-American relationships that I am aware of, both personal and those I have seen in therapy, are far from healthy. Long-standing relationships do exist within the African-American community, but the fact that couples have endured does not mean these relationships are healthy, satisfying, and productive: one can be adjusted in a relationship but not satisfied nor happy with the relationship. For example, take a relationship where spousal abuse occurs. Many women will continue to endure physical and emotional abuse and will remain in the relationship despite everything. Many African-American men are also in abusive relationships in which they endure emotional abuse by their spouses and mates. Relationships like these can often endure for years. Would you refer to these relationships as "healthy" or "productive"? I don't believe you would. My point is that much of what is dysfunctional in the African-American relationship can be credited to the deliberate destruction of the African-American male-female relationship by slave owners, who made a deliberate and intentional effort to destroy the dynamic between the African-American female and the African-American male. The effects of the destruction of the African-American marriage and family can still be observed today. In order to understand the challenges that African-American couples face, it is necessary to be aware of and understand the conditioning process that was implemented upon the African-American female and how this process affected the African-American male-female relationship.

The WLL included instructions on how to make a slave and a collaborator of the African woman: in order to destroy the African-American marital unit, it was necessary that the African-American male be rendered powerless and ineffective in his ability to protect his female. Once this occurred, the African-American female psychologically withdrew her emotional dependence upon him and accepted him as incapable of providing support and protection. The African-American female was on her own to negotiate her own survival and the survival of her offspring. As Lynch stated, she became "psychologically independent...now you got the nigger woman out front and the man behind and scared." Based on my own personal experiences and observations of couples in therapy, it would appear that the slave masters' psychological conditioning to destroy the African-American marriage and relationship was largely successful. The influence of this psychological conditioning involving the dynamics between African-American males and females can still be observed today. There tends to be an interpersonal struggle for control of the relationship among African-American couples. The female is typically not comfortable in these relationships unless she is in charge and in control, yet she demands that her mate take charge and be responsible. Many of the men I see in therapy state that they are frustrated because their wives or mates will not permit them to be responsible and to direct the relationship. It's like a double-edged sword: if the man does attempt to take charge and to exercise control, conflict inevitably results. If he becomes passive and yielding, he is dubbed and viewed as being weak and irresponsible. "What is a poor brother supposed to do?" I am often asked. What I have witnessed is a constant conflict within the marriage or relationship in terms of who will control the relationship. Minor disagreements become major conflicts as a result, and a battle for power and control ensues.

Remember how Lynch stated that the African-American male had to be broken, humiliated, and even killed, all while the female watched? This experience left the African-American female alone and afraid for her own life and for the lives of her children. She consequently learned not to depend on her mate and to psychologically divorce herself from him emotionally. As a result, the African-American female in essence had to fend for herself and not depend on her mate. African-American women therefore assumed control; the slave owner permitted this, because this was just the state of affairs that could ensure his dominance. So for over 465 years the roles of African-American men and women have been reversed. As Lynch suggested, "In her frozen psychological state of independence she will raise her male and female offspring in reversed roles. For fear of the young male's life, she will psychologically train him to be mentally weak and dependent." I witness the continuation of this slave psychology today in the twenty-first century in how mothers raise their sons and in how they interact with their mates. African-American mothers routinely refer to their male children as "their babies" long into adulthood. As cited earlier, according to the National Fatherhood Initiative, two-thirds of African-American children (almost 67 percent) are growing up without the presence of their biological fathers. As a result, numerous women and children in the African-American community lack responsible men in their lives. Although African-American mothers do exist who do a decent job of raising their sons, they still cannot teach a boy how to be a man, nor can they teach a girl how to effectively deal with men. What one most often sees are African-American mothers creating dependency and irresponsibility among their sons. These mothers do not intend that their sons will be irresponsible and dependent, but they unconsciously do just that by referring to them as "their babies" and treating them as if they were unable to be responsible. To put that in a way that most African Americans will be able to relate to, mothers tend to spoil their sons by being overly protective, intrusive, and demeaning whenever the sons attempt to exercise independence. In our counseling practice, we see an untold number of single mothers with adolescent sons who are rebelling against them and being defiant. These mothers bring their sons to counseling for us to "fix" them: to make them more compliant and obedient toward them. What these mothers do not understand is that their sons are rebelling against their unconscious (and sometimes conscious) attempts to psychoemotionally castrate them.

Other African-American mothers resort to "emotional incest." Emotional incest occurs when a mother becomes emotionally dependent upon her son. The male child becomes the surrogate mate to this kind of mother, replacing the man in her life. Many an African-American mother actually refuses to let her sons "grow up" and become men. The son becomes the only predictable male in her life and the only male she can control. If a mother raises her son to be dependent and irresponsible, she can be assured of his devotion and his allegiance only to her. These kinds of mothers are the ones who will actually compete with the girlfriend or wife for her son's control and loyalty to her over the wife or girlfriend. These mothers demand that they be the first priority in their sons' lives. They define their entire lives by controlling and directing their sons' lives. These are the mothers who are often in conflict with the girlfriend or wife; sometimes they even strive to break up the relationship. They are the mothers who "eat" their sons. Often the sons of these mothers develop a host of psychoemotional problems. In an effort to assert their independence, for example, many young African-American males engage in a host of risky and self-injurious behaviors and they tend to form relationships with women who are willing to assume the role of their mothers. Many African-American women whom I know and have had as clients tend to assume ownership of their relationships; they tend to view the relationship as "theirs" exclusively. These African-American women have already defined the role for a man in "their" relationship; if he does not live up to their prescribed role as they've defined it, they become dissatisfied and oppositional. What ensues next is a battle for control over the relationship. Many African-American males become frustrated in their efforts to become the head of the household and simply abandon the relationship or develop dysfunctional methods of coping.

CASE EXAMPLE OF "RODNEY"

"Rodney" is a thirty-seven-year-old African-American male who first came to counseling because he was contemplating suicide. Rodney has been married to the same woman for seventeen years, and they have three children ages sixteen, fourteen and eleven. Rodney spent almost two years in prison for drug charges, and he is now on five years' parole. The fact that he has a felony makes it difficult for him to find employment. Rodney stated that he had attempted suicide about eight years ago by taking fifteen or so Xanax tablets, but he only succeeded in making himself sick for a few days. He stated that he had attempted suicide because his wife of seventeen years had thrown him out of the house. He had been fired from a fast-food management job where he had worked for roughly four years. He stated that he was fired unjustly and because he was African American. Rodney became depressed and angry after losing his job; he began to abuse alcohol and crack cocaine, which made his life even more unmanageable. Rodney worked only occasionally after being fired and spent most of his time unproductively. He was now living with his mother, who did not treat him very well and belittled him. He stated that his mother treated him and his brother harshly while they were growing up. She was demeaning and she often emotionally abused him and his brother by cursing at them in front of friends and relatives. Among other things, she would tell them that they were worthless and that they were no good, just like their father. Rodney stated that his wife was demanding and controlling like his mother, and that in her eyes he could never do anything right.

***

The case example of Rodney is one that is repeated over and over again and represents many African-American men who feel defeated by life. Rodney's mother had taught him to become helpless and ineffective as a man; he stated that he did not have a relationship with his father and that everything he heard about his father was negative. As a result of his upbringing, Rodney had no idea how to assert himself as a man. He was totally unaware of how to manage his life and how to be a husband and father. Rodney further complained that his wife would not let him be a man and that she would defy him and his attempt to be the head of the household. He complained that his wife constantly undermined his authority as a man and struggled with him constantly for power and control within their household.

Another manifestation of the role reversal created by the Lynch method of slave programming involves what is known as the "fifty-fifty" relationship. Many African-American women who do not expect to control their relationships will, however, expect their relationship to be a "fifty-fifty" one in which they will have an equal "say so" in the affairs of the relationship. I have heard this sentiment expressed on countless occasions when conducting marital counseling with African-American couples. Generally the wife believes that she should have equal influence over any matters that pertain to the relationship. I try to explain that there are no "fifty-fifty" relationships, and that most relationships represent a division of labor and responsibility at best. Each partner in a relationship has certain strengths and weaknesses, and responsibilities and tasks should be allocated on this basis. In my own marriage of thirty-five years, for example, we have learned to defer to each other on the basis of our strengths and interests. There are certain things that my wife is better at than I am, while I am better at certain other things than she is. We thus work together to accomplish what the family as a whole needs and requires. There is no competition within the relationship, just cooperation. Many African-American women also believe, however, that if they work and produce an income, they should have a voice that will reflect their income. If a woman earns more money than her mate, she believes she should have the greater input into the affairs of the relationship. In other words, she believes that if she makes the most money, she should have the right to control and dictate the relationship and that her desires should be paramount. In this view, money equals power and control in the relationship.

Unfortunately, the common perception of the role of the husband in America is that of the primary breadwinner: that is, the husband, as the head of the household, is expected to be the primary source of financial support for the family. Sadly, many men in America have subscribed to this definition as defining both what it means to be the head of a household and what it means to be a man.

I have warned many women and men not to fall for this role definition that is based on money and income. In today's world incomes change constantly. In my own marriage, for example, there have been times when my wife earned more money than I did, there were times when I earned more than she did, there were times when she was employed and I was not, and there were times when I was employed and she was not. A relationship has to be defined on mutual goals and cooperation in an effort to sustain the relationship and the family.

CASE EXAMPLE OF "MARY"

"Roy and Mary" had been married for twenty-one years when Mary sought counseling. Mary attended counseling without Roy because she was debating whether she wanted to divorce him or not. She had become very dissatisfied with their marriage. Mary complained that Roy had lost his job and that he had not worked for over a year; as a result, the couple's entire financial burden was placed on her. She further complained that she had always wanted to be a housewife and homemaker but that Roy did not make enough money for them to live as she desired (although he was an engineer and had worked for over twenty years at a large engineering company). Roy and Mary had one child, who was eighteen years of age and had just graduated from high school and was enrolling in college. Mary considered Roy to be dead weight she did not need, especially since their daughter was now grown and in college. Mary earned a very good income working as an executive assistant to a vice-president of a large company. Mary had no other complaints about Roy except that he was very religious and had to pray about everything. She felt that he was not aggressive enough and that he was passive in his approach to life, and she wanted more. Mary felt that Roy was now holding her back from enjoying her life.

After three sessions with Mary, I advised her that she had insufficient grounds for wanting to divorce Roy, because on all accounts he was a decent, God-fearing, hardworking man who was doing his best to provide for the family. I later asked Roy to come to counseling, and he did. I learned that Roy was truly a "good" man. He was God-fearing, honest, and faithful, and a gentleman on all accounts. Roy stated that he was confused by his wife's attitude and her actions toward him. He knew she was dissatisfied about his unemployment status; he stated that he was searching for another job but that he believed his age may have hindered his efforts. When I saw Mary again, I cautioned her to reconsider her intentions to divorce Roy. In my opinion, I did not believe that she had any moral grounds to divorce Roy and that his state of unemployment was temporary. Mary had already made up her mind to divorce him, however, and did so a few months later. About six months later, Roy contacted me for a counseling appointment. He informed me that he had obtained another job where he made more money than he had at his previous job. He told me that during the divorce, the house had been sold and the money had been divided between himself and Mary. Roy then informed me that Mary had lost her job and was now very distraught and depressed because things had backfired on her. Roy stated that Mary was too ashamed to face him and that she had rejected his efforts to help her. I never heard from Mary again.

***

This case example is a good one of what can happen when the basis for a relationship is based on money alone. There is much more to a marriage and a relationship than money. Money is not a basis for power and control in a relationship. A couple has to define the purpose for their relationship and then work together to achieve the mutual goals of the relationship. African Americans have to reverse the roles back to their natural order. The man is the natural head of the household, with the wife as his helpmate and not his dictate, as I like to say. A question I ask women in counseling all the time is this: If someone breaks into your home, what do you expect your husband or mate to do? In every case they respond by saying that they expect their husband or mate to handle the situation and to protect them and the family. I jokingly say to these women, "Why don't you face the intruder and protect your husband and your family?" They always respond that it is the man's job to protect them. At this juncture I believe I have made my point. I further explain that it is instinctual for a man to risk or give his life if necessary for his wife and his family without any hesitation. There is no "fifty-fifty" in this situation. Men will listen to their women, but men do not want to be dictated to or struggle with their women for power and control in the relationship. I ask women this question routinely in my counseling practice: What does a woman represent in the life of a man? I have never received a correct answer to this question. I then pose the question to these women that if they do not know what a woman represents in the life of a man or why he wants a woman in his life, then how can she ever hope to satisfy a man? Many women believe that the man's job is to satisfy and please their mate. I suggest that a woman represents a source of comfort and pleasure for a man and that this is why he wants a woman in his life. I further warn women that when they stop being comfortable and pleasurable to be with, he will more than likely leave them. Men do battle with the world, and they don't want to come home and do battle again. In many African-American relationships, however, there tends to be a battle for power and control. This trend has to be changed, and the natural order has to be restored. African-American men have to learn how to be the head of household and be assertive, and African-American women have to learn how to be supportive without being defiant and controlling. This reversal of male and female roles has to be restored to the natural order in the African-American male-female relationship. This role reversal created during slavery continues to create difficulty and conflict among African-American relationships.

CASE EXAMPLE OF "DAN"

It is my practice when counseling couples to see each spouse individually first and then have the couple attend counseling together after I have seen each of them separately. In this case Dan attended counseling first. Dan complained that his wife was controlling and demanding of him, as if he were a child. Dan explained that his wife was a few years older than he was and that she treated him like a child rather than a man. He stated that he could never satisfy her and that she complained when he would not take the lead in their affairs. Before he could respond to her requests, she would take the initiative and then complain that he was unreliable. Dan stated that she would not give him the chance to respond to their needs or their family affairs and that she would always preempt him in things. Dan stated that he felt like they were competing for power and control in their relationship and that he was losing. At this point I have to state that Dan was a white man. I had not yet met his wife. The following week, Dan's wife came to counseling for her initial counseling session. To my surprise, she was an African-American woman. I had not considered that Dan's wife might be African American. I now understood what Dan was complaining about. When I saw Dan at his next counseling session, I told him that he was experiencing what many African-American husbands were experiencing with their wives and mates. I had to explain the historical dynamics involved to Dan so that he could gain a perspective about his experiences with being married to an African-American woman. I told him not to take it personally and to understand that his wife had been psychologically programmed to behave the way she was toward him and their relationship. Dan seemed relieved that he was not doing anything wrong.

***

These are just a few examples of the dilemmas that African Americans face in their quest for healthy marriages and relationships. Without a doubt, Willie Lynch's destructive influence in the lives of African Americans can still be observed today. As Lynch warned, "the mind has a strong drive to correct and to recorrect itself over time." The first step toward psychological health is to first become aware and to recognize the presence of OPD-I and how African Americans have developed this disorder as a result of slavery and oppression. Most African Americans are not consciously aware of the effects of the Lynch system of psychological slave programming that affects their efforts to engage in healthy and productive relationships. Most of what I have described occurs at the unconscious level. This is why I use the Willie Lynch Letter as part of my therapeutic approach. After couples have read the part pertaining to the "Negro Marriage Unit," they are able to instantly recognize how they have been programmed to function in their relationship; they are then able to begin modifying their behaviors toward one another and how they view their relationship. Without this information, African-American men and women resort to coping with their relationship in several dysfunctional ways. For example, African-American men will resort to the use of drugs and alcohol as a way to cope with their relationship. Other African-American men will simply abandon the relationship or engage in infidelity, some will opt for women of another race, some will resort to violence, and others will seek separation and divorce. African-American women, in contrast, will most often seek separation and divorce as a first option. Some African-American women will develop lesbian relationships; some will develop homoemotional relationships (these are the women who join the NAS club). Some African-American women will settle for a dependent and irresponsible mate in order to have and maintain control in the relationship, which conforms to the Willie Lynch formula. A few African-American women will opt for men of another race. Currently these coping styles are reflective of how African-American men and women are attempting to cope and deal with their dysfunctional interpersonal relationships. In order to correct this current situation between African-American men and African-American women, a complete understanding of the dynamics involved in the undoing and the reversal of the male-female roles across generations of African Americans must first be recognized and understood.

OPD-I and Child Rearing

African Americans must begin to raise their children with an understanding of their purpose in life if they are going to be successful and find personal fulfillment in life. I have already discussed the importance of history. Without this knowledge of history, African-American children will continue to be influenced by others who seek to oppress and mislead them. African Americans cannot afford to raise their children and youth in the same way that white people rear their children. They must not emulate the same standards, beliefs, and values that white parents use to raise their children. For the most part, white parents raise their children with a laissez-faire approach; in other words, they tend to be liberal and tolerant of undisciplined behavior and to maintain a hands-off attitude. It is well documented that white society, by and large, does not believe in spanking or whipping their children. They permit their children to be defiant and oppositional and nonconforming for a reason. You have to understand that whites do not intend their children to grow up and respect any authority other than themselves. African Americans cannot afford to have the same liberal attitude as whites do in raising their children. African Americans have to prepare their youth for the inevitable struggle that will face them during their lifetimes. In order to be successful, African-American children will have to be self-disciplined; they must be self-directed and they must have a strong sense of purpose.

As of this writing, many African-American youth have no sense of purpose for their lives. Many African-American youth of today have little respect for themselves and little to no respect for others, let alone their ancestors. African Americans today are raising a generation of ignorant, disrespectful, and ungrateful youth. In our work with youth in the juvenile-justice system, we often hear youths declare that no one can tell them what to do. Yet when these same youths are standing in front of a white judge, they behave as if they have good sense. While they are respectful and speak with consideration in such situations, at this point it is too late to behave with self-discipline. African Americans must understand that the "system" will accommodate the misbehaving white child. In other words, white children will not be punished for their youthful mistakes and their lack of conformity. We witness on a daily basis white youth committing the same violations of the law and the rules but facing little in the way of consequence. When an African-American youth misbehaves or violates the rules or the law, in contrast, he or she is going to be punished to the fullest extent possible. In other words, the system is not going to accommodate African-American youth as it would white youth.

African Americans need to understand that different standards are applied to their children and youth. For example, take the case of the six-year-old girl in Florida who was arrested by the police for essentially being a child. She was arrested and handcuffed because she would not comply with her white teachers, who in my observation continued to provoke her. African Americans must understand that the agenda of white society is to force compliance and to maintain control, especially when it comes to African-American males. This is why African Americans must discipline their children early and help them understand the hostile environment they will have to negotiate. African Americans believe their children can act and behave as white children do; as a consequence of this belief, African-American parents set their children up for failure and punishment. African-American parents have to realize that the system will accommodate white children, yet the same system will punish theirs. African-American parents thus have to prepare their children to deal with an oppressive and punitive system. I have witnessed unassuming African-American parents tell their children that they do not have to obey anyone or any adult other than themselves. These children and youth generally fail to obey their parents as well. African Americans cannot continue to be blind to the impact of their ill-informed practices on their children, because they undermine and ultimately destroy their children. The manifestation of these actions of African-American parents makes them collaborators by cooperating with an oppressive agenda to destroy their children.

Another area of concern is the failure to teach African-American youth an appreciation for work. Low-income African-American parents teach their children how to survive without working and how to avoid work. I am referring to the intergenerational welfare recipient who has developed a welfare mentality: a mentality that has its roots in OPD-I. These are the African Americans who try to "get over" on the system. These are the African Americans who steal for a living, sell drugs and sex, live on welfare, disability payments, and "crazy checks"—anything to avoid legitimate work and employment. The children and youth of these parents are taught how to avoid work. In their mind, work is for suckers and squares. They believe their effort to avoid work is smart. These misguided African Americans hold two of what Albert Ellis and Catharine MacLaren refer to as "irrational beliefs" in their 1998 book *Rational Emotive Behavior Therapy*: that "happiness means having nothing to do" and "life should be without pain and require little effort."

Some middle-class and upper-income parents also fail to instill in their children a strong value and a strong respect for work. Many middle- and upper-income African-American parents have said to me that they do not want their children to struggle and experience the same difficulties and hardships they experienced. As a result, these parents tend to overindulge their children and raise them with a false illusion that life should be easy and that they do not have to put forth much effort to achieve success in life. We have had talked to hundreds of middle- and upper-income African-American youth who are failing in school and trying to emulate the "gangster-ghetto" lifestyle. These are the African-American youth who aspire to become thugs or attempt to emulate privileged white youth. Either way, these middle- to upper-income African-American youth fail to appreciate their unique circumstances in life. They have the best of everything that money can buy, but they do not appreciate the sacrifices their parents have made because their parents want to shelter them from the harsh reality of having to struggle and sacrifice; they want to shelter their children from what it means to be African American. Middle- and upper-income African-American parents who are unaware of their purpose in life cannot convey to their children a sense of purpose. These African-American parents create a sense of entitlement and unearned privilege in their children. As a consequence, many of these African-American youth fail to survive and thrive because they don't know how to work and they do not appreciate work. These are the African-American youth who behave and sound like sick white kids. I am personally familiar with several African-American families whose teenaged sons have never mowed their lawns; instead, they have a yardman who does the work. I began teaching my own son at an early age how to cut the grass and how to do other work involving manual labor. My belief and rationale is that I had to instill in my son an appreciation for work and a willingness to work. As a result and he has learned the value of work and has developed a strong work ethic.

Too many middle- and upper-income African-American parents fail their children by giving them everything they want without demanding anything of them in return. It is my practice and my belief that children should earn money for the things they want. As a result of this belief, I have provided my own children with the opportunity to earn money. Teenagers learn several things when they can earn money for the things they want. The first thing they learn is that they must work to receive money. They learn the value of money, they learn how to manage money, they learn to become self-reliant, and they learn how to perform and how to complete a task; indeed, working improves their self-concept and self-esteem. I cannot overemphasize the value of teaching a child to value work. I have witnessed many children from middle- and upper-income homes who fail to perpetuate the gains that their parents made because their parents overindulged them and did not teach them the value of work. My son and I are the only father/son duo in our neighborhood who cut our own grass. When we cut our grass, our neighbors look at us with a curious and perplexed look. One neighbor asked one day why I didn't have a yardman, because he knew I could afford one. I explained that I was teaching my son a skill he could use to make a living if he had to and that I was teaching him to appreciate the fact that he had a yard to care for. I also explained to my neighbor that cutting my own grass also provided me with the exercise I needed. African Americans must prepare their children for the real world they will face and not permit them to waste their time and waste their minds. Since the majority of African Americans are Christian and profess to believe in the Bible, African Americans should obey the Bible and use corporal punishment during the early years. The scriptures are clear about how to discipline a child. As a result of OPD-I, however, African-American parents want to emulate whites in raising their children. It is this tendency by African Americans parents to emulate whites in their child-rearing practices that contributes to the failure of their children.

GHETTO GONE MAINSTREAM

Rap music and hip-hop have together proven to be the greatest social influence on African-American culture over the last twenty-five years. Rap music began as an art form that provided a generation of young African Americans an avenue of self-expression. Rap began innocently enough as poetic expression of experiences and emotions. Of course, rap was nothing new as an art form. What is today known as "rap" began in the late 1960s with artists such as Nikki Giovanni and the Last Poets. The term "rap" as a label for this particular art form, however, first occurred in the early 1980s. Young people began to embrace this form of poetic expression. The term "rap" was initially used during the 1960s by the hippie counterculture. During this time, to rap meant to talk (e.g., "Let's rap"). People rapped with one another. Of course, each generation believes it has discovered something new and unique that defines them. Regardless of its origin, rap has taken over popular culture over the last twenty-five years. While rap as an art form is not in itself problematic, rap evolved during the late 1980s into a vehicle to deliver to young people the most destructive life orientation ever witnessed in history. This new brand of "gangster rap" served to undermine at least three generations of young people, especially young African Americans. Gangster rap glamorized gang violence, sex, drugs, and general defiance. Young African Americans began to embrace this new form of self-destruction as a path to quick wealth and fame. Entrepreneurs in the music industry seized this opportunity to capitalize by promoting would-be life failures into icons. Young African Americans were deluded into believing that by embracing the gangster rap lifestyle, they could achieve their dreams and aspirations of wealth and freedom. As a consequence, young African Americans abandoned self-discipline and self-respect for this seemingly glamorous and irresponsible lifestyle: one that promised to fulfill all their aspirations. The glamorization of the gangster rap lifestyle resulted in a segment of young African Americans abandoning the traditional values of education, honest work, and a general respect for societal values. Entrepreneurs in the music industry sought out and promoted the most banal young African American they could find. It was good business for the powers at large, but it was destructive to several generations of young African Americans.

As a result of promoting the most banal individuals to iconic status, young people now aspired to being "ghetto" and all that goes along with it. Middle- and upper-class young people aspired to be ghetto, not realizing that these so-called gangster rappers were trying to get out of the ghetto by selling them the biggest load of manure of all time. This countercultural phenomenon has resulted in a lifestyle that encourages sexual promiscuity, oppositional defiance toward authority (parents, school officials, and law enforcement, among others), drug activity, and related issues. This great deception afflicted many African-American youth with a culture of oppositional defiance and conduct disorder at some level, creating a disregard for the values that have permitted African Americans to survive for hundreds of years: the rapid movement toward self-destruction and self-annihilation that was a continuation and a deepening of "the phenomena of illusions" described in the WLL.

CASE EXAMPLE OF "MICHAEL"

One Thursday afternoon I went to a drug store to buy a few personal items. As I approached the entrance to the drug store, I saw a young man standing near the entrance. As I approached he asked me for some spare change. I did not respond and entered the store. As I was about to pay for the items, I realized I had left my wallet in my car. I placed the items on the counter and left the store to retrieve my wallet. The young man asked me again for some change. On my way to the car I decided I would give this young man some change once I left the store. Something about this young man caught my attention. I felt a sort of empathy for him and wanted to help him if I could. He represented so many young African-American men that I see and encounter almost daily. I was curious about his life story and why he was begging for change. This young man was about six feet two inches in height and appeared to be at least 180 pounds. He appeared to be in good health, with no obvious handicap. As I exited the store, I handed him about $1.50 in change. After giving him the change, I asked him his name. He told me his name was Michael. I asked his age, and he responded that he was thirty-two. I asked him why he was in front of the store begging for money. He told me he was getting money for food and needed a place to sleep for the night because his spot in the homeless shelter had been assigned to someone else. I asked why he was in a homeless shelter in the first place. He told me his situation was only temporary, because "he was just waiting for his record deal to come through." He told me that he was a rapper and had signed with a record company but was waiting for the government to finalize the deal. At this point I knew he was delusional. He told me that he was an important person and that he had some movie scripts and some other material that were going to make him a star and that everyone would see him on TV and the movies. I then asked him if he had any illnesses or any kind of physical disability. He told me that he was in good health. I then asked him why didn't get a job while he was waiting for his record deal to come through. He told me that he had tried to get a job, but the jobs were controlled by the system and that "they" were a part of the demon conspiracy to control the black man and he did not want any part of it. He further stated that he had to stay in place so that when his record deal was approved he would be available. It was obvious this young man had bought into the illusion of the rap culture, believing that his ticket to wealth and fame was to become a rapper. To make matters worse, this young man was using drugs that helped deepen his illusion of becoming a famous rapper.

***

The sad thing about Michael is that he is a mere example of untold numbers of young African-American youth who have been deceived and misdirected by the popular rap lifestyle. Michael is a lost soul without any sense of reality. Because his illusion is so profound, I fear he may never return to reality. The rap and hip-hop lifestyle requires little in terms of self-discipline and responsibility. It is attractive for many youth, because they don't really have to do anything beyond posturing. Unfortunately, many misguided African-American youth believe the prerequisites for becoming a successful rap artist are experiencing incarceration, being shot or shooting someone, being involved in drugs, being affiliated with a gang, and engaging in sexual promiscuity. In other words, they believe they have to have "street cred" in order to be a legitimate rap artist, however crazy that sounds. It is interesting that the majority of youth I have worked with believe I don't know anything because I don't have street experience, as if I had been born on a different planet.

Another sad thing I frequently witness is that it takes young African Americans until about the age of forty before they begin to come to terms with reality. African Americans already suffer from the illusions created by slavery and oppression, and now there is a greater gulf to overcome created by the illusionary world of rap and hip-hop. As the rap and hip-hop lifestyle fails to produce all that is promised, young people become angry, frustrated, and desperate to fulfill their aspirations. This anger and frustration often lead these young people into a life of crime and drug use and dealing. Out of desperation, many young African Americans resort to antisocial behavior. Many find it difficult or impossible to redirect their efforts in a positive and productive way because they have sacrificed their education and have failed to acquire any employable skills. Unfocused and undisciplined, these casualties of the rap movement live in a perpetual world of illusion, floating ever further from reality. There was a time when ignorant, uneducated, unskilled, inexperienced African Americans understood their social and economic standing. Today, however, lesser accomplished African Americans take issue with those in their community who clearly outrank them and are in a position to assist them. In other words, there has developed a general disrespect and a general disregard for traditional values that involve self-discipline, self-respect, and hard work. This general disregard for traditional values is a direct result of the rap and hip-hop movement, which has elevated banality and hedonism as the model for young African Americans to aspire to.

The first way an individual learns in life is through imitation. At some point in life, one has to begin to think for oneself and begin to engage in critical thinking; but it is easier to just imitate others. Unfortunately, too many young African Americans are imitating what they see on television and in videos and magazines. If you ask these young people why they tattoo themselves, pierce themselves, wear their pants off their asses, use drugs, drop out of school, commit crimes, dye their hair red, blue, or green, and so on, they will tell you that they are just being themselves and expressing their unique individuality. If you confront them with the fact that they are merely imitating others, they become almost belligerent. The sad fact is that they are imitating others whom they hold in high esteem as role models. It is sad that this group of young African Americans will not imitate people of substance and accomplishment. If you ask them who and what they represent with their actions, they cannot tell you. You see, it is easier to imitate and create an image than it is to apply oneself. Many young African Americans have opted for imitating an image rather than working toward advancement through education and disciplined work. Many young African Americans have developed what is known as "work inhibition." Work inhibition is the avoidance of work in the traditional sense. As in the case of Michael, he could not bring himself to consider any kind of traditional work. He justified his avoidance of work by offering conspiracy and discrimination theories. Michael believed that working a regular job would somehow jeopardize his efforts to become a rapper. It was obvious that Michael had created an illusion for himself that he fully embraced; he will probably remain within his illusion for the remainder of his life.

CASE EXAMPLE OF "JOAN"

"Joan" is a twenty-six-year-old African-American female with three children, and she is pregnant with her fourth. Each of her children has different fathers except for the first two children. Joan had her first child at age sixteen. Her first boyfriend, or "baby daddy," Johnny, was eighteen when he met Joan. He was an aspiring rapper and a drug dealer. He had big dreams of becoming a rapper and owning his own record label. Joan joined him in his illusionary aspirations and saw herself as "the girlfriend" of this soon-to-be famous rapper. Well, as the story often goes, Johnny was arrested for drug dealing and various other violations of the law and ended up being sentenced to fifteen years in prison. Joan became a topless dancer to support herself and her child. She met another "gangster" at the strip club and became involved with this man, who was also arrested and sentenced to prison, but not before getting her pregnant. Joan now lives in public housing with public assistance. She has not tried to get an education or to work at a regular job. She continues to wait for her "knight in shining armor." She has little ambition, and she suffers from depression, with frequent thoughts of suicide.

***

Over the years I have heard many similar stories from African-American youth, who hold several common illusions. For young African-American males, there is the NFL illusion, the NBA illusion, the drug-dealer illusion, and the rapper illusion, to name a few. The aspiration to become an NFL or NBA professional ballplayer does become a reality for a very few who have talent and discipline and remain in school. I have talked with youth who are not in school and who lack the mental or physical ability to become professional athletes but who actually believe that they can become professional ballplayers. I will never forget "Kendrick." Kendrick was a drug-using, fourteen-year-old dropout who stood about five foot four inches tall and weighed 129 pounds. When I asked what he wanted to become, he told me he wanted to become an NBA star. I realized he was suffering from a severe illusion and was completely unaware of the requirements to become an NBA professional. He had a profoundly unrealistic view of himself and his abilities.

To make matters worse, society tends to foster and reinforce these illusions. It is interesting that the highest-paid people are those who are involved in nonessential occupations. What I mean by "nonessential occupations" are those occupations that have little to no fundamental value in terms of sustaining society and individuals. For example, if all the ballplayers and entertainers were to disappear tomorrow, the world would not come to an end. People would entertain themselves, and they would make their own music and devise their own games for amusement. In America the most nonessential occupations are paid the most. Is it any wonder that young people do not see and understand the value of getting an education? Teachers and college professors are among the least-paid professionals. The average income for surgeons is a mere $187,000 a year. There is almost an inverse relationship between the amount of education and the amount of money earned. Unfortunately, young African Americans aspire to become involved in these nonessential professions as a way of achieving fame and fortune. The problem is that most will become casualties in the pursuit of their illusions. I am afraid that in another two generations, young African Americans will not be able to differentiate reality from illusion. The illusions are becoming elaborate and more profound. The great Booker T. Washington (1901) proposed a solution for the plight of African Americans. His solution was simple. He stated that the African American "should obtain an education and learn a skill, buy land and save money." His advice is still sound today. Instead of learning a skill and getting an education, too many young African Americans are dropping out of school and selling drugs. Instead of saving money and buying land, they are buying used cars and spending their money on twenty-two-inch rims and tires and living in apartments or living with their Section 8 baby mommas. As Willie Lynch stated, "the mind has a strong drive to correct and recorrect itself over a period of time if it can touch original historical base." Well, young and old African Americans alike are moving further from an understanding of their history and moving further into illusions, as

Willie Lynch stated. As long as African Americans are ignorant of their history, others will always appear superior to them.

Chapter IV: The Path to Psychological Recovery

The Solution: A Blueprint for Achieving Psychological Health

OPD-I permeates every single aspect of African-American life. Regardless of income, education, age, or sex, OPD-I is present in the thoughts and behaviors of practically all African Americans at some level. No matter their socioeconomic level, OPD-I tends to be operating. If African Americans as a people are going to continue moving forward in their quest for complete freedom and independence, they are going to have to address and correct the 465 years of psychological programming that has occurred and that is still in effect today. African Americans will have to recognize the ways they have become self-destructive and dysfunctional before they can achieve their personal goals and aspirations as well as their collective goals and aspirations. African Americans must understand that many of their personal goals and aspirations stand the best chance of being fulfilled if they first become united in their efforts. African Americans must appreciate the fact that they are stronger as a united people working together. Therefore, this writing is an attempt to stimulate thought, research, and dialogue and ultimately to help devise a solution to correct the effects of slavery and oppression at the psychological level. The chains have been removed from the body, but the chains remain on the minds of African Americans. The first step is for African Americans to become aware of how they have been psychologically programmed. Therefore, African Americans have to begin healing themselves by becoming conscious of their own behaviors and thoughts. For the first time in history, African Americans have the opportunity to be self-governing and self-directed as individuals and as a people. Unfortunately, African Americans did not have a well-defined agenda beyond 1964 once they achieved complete rights under the laws of the United States of America. As a result of not having a collective agenda beyond this point, African Americans have digressed and regressed into the pursuit of individual agendas and integration. There have been many articles and books that discuss the strengths of African Americans and the African-American family. However, there has been a conscious or maybe an unconscious tendency by African Americans in academia to avoid discussing the dysfunctional behaviors of African American in general. It is my contention that unless African Americans define and discuss the origin and nature of their behavioral dysfunctions, they will remain ineffective in dealing with the various issues that confront them and their community.

Understanding Purpose as an African American

The healthy African-American mind is one that can articulate purpose as an African American. The psychologically healthy African American will seek to integrate the past with the present. Once the past is integrated with the present, the future can be determined. Without this integration of the past with the present, the future will remain unclear. Several years ago I began to ask African-American clients what they believed to be their purpose in life. Most of the responses to this question tended to be a statement of individual goals instead of a purpose. I received answers such as *to be the best person I can and to have a good life, to be successful, to help others*, and *to do God's will*; many responded by saying that they didn't know what their purpose in life was and that it was a question they had been seeking an answer to. In other words, they did not know the difference between a purpose and a goal. Without a significant understanding of African-American history, it is impossible for African Americans to know their purpose in life and who they are as African Americans. Again, this is why knowledge of African-American history is so important, because purpose for African Americans can only be understood in terms of African-American history. It is African-American history that defines life's purpose for African Americans. Healthy African-American minds understand that they are part of a continuum and that their purpose is to continue their ancestors' quest for freedom. Many African Americans today do not understand that their purpose is to continue the quest for life, liberty, and the pursuit of happiness that was denied to their ancestors.

Healthy African-American minds understand that they are soldiers in an ongoing war for power and self-sufficiency; African Americans are still powerless in terms of economics and politics. Healthy African-American minds understand that it is their turn to contribute to the collective good of the African-American community. Healthy African-American minds realize that, collectively, African Americans are still dependent on their oppressors both economically and politically. African Americans with healthy minds are those who seek to empower themselves for the sake of the African-American community and not just for themselves. Healthy African-American minds know and understand that their personal achievements are realized by the contributions of other African Americans who came before them; they know that they are the benefactors of opportunity created by their ancestors. Their success is not wholly the result of their lone singular efforts, as many African Americans tend to mistakenly believe. Healthy African-American minds realize that any personal achievement was made possible by the sacrifices of their African-American ancestors, and was not due to their own efforts alone. Healthy African-American minds therefore understand that they owe a debt to those who came before them, that they have an obligation to pave the way for those who follow them, and that their personal success and achievements are connected to a larger cause that is greater than themselves. They realize and are appreciative of the fact that their personal success and achievements have been built on the suffering and sacrifices of other great African Americans who came before them. The main characteristic of healthy African-American minds, however, is an understanding of their purpose as soldiers in the ongoing war against oppression and continued struggle for freedom and justice that has been so long denied. Healthy African-American minds understand the clarion call to prepare, to serve, and to ensure the survival of fellow African Americans.

The only thing African Americans have in common is their history in America. History is the only thing that binds African Americans together as a people. If African Americans are not knowledgeable of their history, then they will be unaware of their common purpose. Without an intimate knowledge of their history, African Americans have no bases of relating to one another and, thus, a lack of common purpose.

Based on observations of the behavior of African Americans today, it would appear that African Americans have lost all sense of purpose for their lives. As a group, African Americans today have been taught and psychologically conditioned to be self-destructive and dysfunctional in a manner previously unknown among African Americans as a people. It would appear that African Americans today have lost all sense of mutual respect and self-respect. My experiences with many African-American youth and adults have been disappointing and depressing. Many African-American people—both youths and adults—have little or no understanding of their history; as a consequence they have no clue about their purpose in life or any perspective for their future. When we interview the parents of these youth, however, we discover that the parents of these children have no idea about their purpose as African Americans and that they themselves have little or no knowledge of African-American history. It is the role and job of the parent and the African-American community at large to guide the young. But if the parents have no idea of what their life should mean, it will be impossible for them to convey a sense of purpose to their children.

Practically every day we see African-American parents in our facility bringing their children for counseling and treatment. The majority of these youth are referred to us by the truancy courts, the juvenile department, the state youth commission, and private referrals by insurance companies. Regardless of the source of the referral, one thing remains constant: parents have not conveyed to their children any understanding of what their lives should mean as a person and as an African American. When I ask parents what they have told their children about their purpose in life, they appear to be lost and confused about what I am referring to. Some try to respond by telling me that they have told their children that they should grow up to be successful and to live good lives. I then explain that all parents want their children to have good lives and to be successful. The next question I ask these parents is to define what exactly they mean by a "good life" and "success." Again I witness confusion and frustration when the parents begin to respond to these questions; many will say that they have not really thought about it that way. By this time I have made my point: that as parents they have not provided their children with a sense of purpose and direction beyond a very general and abstract idea of being successful.

At this point I often ask the parents of these youth what their purpose in life is. Again I get the same general response of uncertainty and confusion. The more honest parents will tell me that they don't know what their purpose is and that this is something they themselves want to know. Often, African-American parents will tell me that their purpose in life and the purpose for their child's life is "to do God's work." But they cannot tell me specifically what work God has in mind for them. To know African-American history is to discover your purpose as an African American. Without an understanding of one's history, one's life has little significant meaning or purpose. African Americans must begin to embrace their history if they can hope to correct the current dysfunctional behaviors and destructive tendencies that hinder African Americans today. The system uses ignorance of African-American history as a primary weapon and tactic to keep African Americans under control; it has gone to great lengths to hide the truth about African-American history. Anyone who has any knowledge of American history as taught by the public schools would immediately see and understand that the role of African Americans, Native Americans, and others have been omitted and/or distorted. The "Making of a Slave" section of the WLL includes a warning to the slave owners: "For they say the mind has a strong drive to correct and to recorrect itself over a period of time. If it can touch substantial original historical base; and they advised us to shave off the brute's [black person's] mental history and create a multiplicity of phenomena of illusions."

The primary purpose of African Americans is to continue the struggle for freedom that their ancestors began over four hundred years ago. This struggle began with the fight to secure freedom from slavery. The struggle against oppression of freedom in all of its subtle forms still continues today. It is necessary that African Americans be reminded that it has only been fifty years since African Americans realized freedom under the law in America. Slavery ended in the year 1865 with the end of the Civil War, but it would take another hundred years to obtain the same rights under the law that white Americans enjoyed. It took a lot of fighting and struggle by our African-American forefathers and foremothers to achieve rights under the law. As noted earlier, it wasn't until the passage of the CRA in 1964 and the VRA in 1965 that African Americans began to enjoy the same rights under the law as white

Americans. Many African Americans today behave as if their struggle for freedom is over and that all the barriers to freedom have been eliminated. Many African Americans want to believe there is no longer a need for them to be concerned with oppression and discrimination; indeed, many African Americans seek to forget their collective past struggle for freedom and equality. Some African Americans attempt to disassociate themselves from their painful, but glorious history by trying to assimilate into white society and denying their past. African Americans must follow the example of the Jews, who were slaughtered and persecuted for simply being Jews. The Jews vowed to never forget this aspect of their history. They vowed to remember so that it will not happen again. The Jews therefore teach their children their common history so that their children may continue their vigilance against any oppression and hatred of their people. African Americans, for their part, must never forget their past and the struggle for freedom that has been with them from the beginning of their experience in America. African Americans must understand that the struggle for freedom is not over: it still demands that they remain vigilant. African Americans must embrace this mission and must pass this agenda along to their children. African Americans must understand the many subtle and overt manifestations of racism and oppression as they exist today. The primary agenda or purpose of African Americans is to establish economic power as a community, just as Jewish Americans have done. African Americans must end their economic dependency on others; they must become self-reliant as a community and establish economic power in doing so.

The Importance of History

The first and perhaps most crucial step toward psychological health for an African American will be to study and learn African-American history in detail. One question to be answered is to determine the characteristics of the healthy African-American mind: What represents a healthy thought process for the African American? It has been my experience that in order for an African American to have a healthy state of mind, the first requirement is a strong identification with his or her history along with an intimate understanding of African-American history. In addition to a strong identification with African-American history, African Americans must be able to place themselves on the historical continuum: in other words, they must be able to interpret their own personal circumstances from a historical perspective. Healthy African-American minds understand how African-American history has contributed to their present rights, freedoms, and opportunities. Healthy African-American minds have, and demonstrate, an appreciation for all African Americans who have contributed to the war for freedom; they understand the sacrifices that people made to ensure that future generations of African Americans would enjoy what they could not—freedom and liberty. Healthy African-American minds pay homage to the great leaders of the past and will honor their contributions and hold sacred their legacy. This is exactly the state of affairs for the majority of African Americans today. In a survey we conducted using the aforementioned PDSAA, 100 percent of African Americans stated that they believed it was important to know their own history. When we interviewed and questioned these same African Americans, however, less than 2 percent had read Booker T. Washington, DuBois, Douglass, Malcolm X, Tubman, and so forth. This result highlights one of the main problems for many African Americans: a lack of knowledge of their own history. In order to become a psychologically healthy African American, an intimate knowledge of African-American history is essential; learning this history represents the first step toward achieving psychological health for African Americans.

Many African Americans who do not have an intimate understanding of African-American history live under an illusion, as Lynch referred to it. Without an understanding of African-American history, there is nothing substantial by which African Americans can define themselves. As I have learned, however, many African Americans have no real knowledge of their history. This is why one can observe many African Americans attempting to buy an identity or trying desperately to identify with Anglo-American icons. Identity issues are common among the African-American population, which is representative of OPD-I: the "Michael Jackson" phenomenon discussed earlier. Many African Americans I have encountered have become highly vested in their illusions and will defend their particular illusion with great fervor. I have experienced many African Americans who became angry and hostile at the questioning of their identity or when they felt that the validity of their illusion was being challenged. I would say that most African Americans do not know who they are; they merely imitate some aspect of the majority culture. An intimate knowledge of African-American history is necessary as a first step toward achieving psychological health and a healthy identity as a person in general. Again, the question remains: What is the purpose for African Americans in American society today? Another question that needs to be asked is if there is a unique common purpose for African Americans. It is my belief that in order to answer these questions, African Americans must first examine (and fully understand and appreciate) their history as African Americans. It is that knowledge and appreciation of African-American history that gives meaning and significance to the African-American existence. By understanding the past, African Americans can understand the present and the direction they should follow in the future. African Americans, like all people, are defined by their history. Only an understanding of history can help define the present and therefore the future for any people. African Americans must therefore first develop an appreciation of their unique history in order to properly and accurately define their purpose in life, which is to continue the long-standing struggle for life, liberty, and the pursuit of happiness.

There is no denying the fact that much of African-American history is painful and is difficult to reconcile for many African Americans. As a result, many African Americans attempt to avoid thinking about and learning about their own history. While much of African-American history is indeed painful, much of it also represents a source of great pride and strength. The history of any people contains both positive and negative aspects, but too many African Americans fail to embrace the positive aspects of their history in their attempts to avoid the negative aspects of it. In my personal experience, I have found that many African Americans tend to concentrate on either the negative aspects exclusively or they tend to focus on the positive aspects only. African Americans must learn to accept and embrace the entirety of African-American history. A balanced and thorough understanding of African-American history is necessary if African Americans are to develop a healthy personal identity.

Much of African-American history is excluded from the textbooks that children study in school. Today's textbooks might include a brief section or a few paragraphs pertaining to African Americans as a part of American history. Even college textbooks exclude any significant discussion of African-American historical facts. The adoption of a history textbook for use in public schools in Texas was recently defeated because the book referred to slavery as "an unpaid internship." How outrageous is this effort to minimize the severity of slavery? Some colleges and universities do offer courses in African-American history, but the majority of African Americans will never be exposed to these opportunities to learn about their own history. Black History Month is the only time during the year that African-American children are exposed to their history in a somewhat organized way. While advocates have launched efforts to get state legislatures to pass legislation that would require school districts to teach African-American history in schools, to date only four states have done so. African Americans cannot expect others to teach their history to them or indeed to place any importance on it. It is African Americans' responsibility to learn and then to teach their history to their children. A thorough knowledge of African-American history is an essential component of the personal development of the African American as a psychologically healthy individual. Without the knowledge of their history, African Americans will be incomplete as individuals and as a people. Understanding and appreciating African-American history is essential in establishing a sense of purpose in African Americans' daily lives.

One thing that binds all African Americans together is their history and experience in America. African Americans must understand their contributions throughout American history that have helped America become the most powerful and wealthy nation on earth. Many would argue that without the forced labor and exploitation of African Americans, America would not have become the great nation that it is today. African-American males, in particular, have contributed to the greatness of America like no other group in the history of America. African Americans must therefore not let their history go untold and unknown. It is vitally important for every African American to know and to become intimate with their great history if they are to understand their future destiny and their present purpose. Once again, remember Lynch's words: "shave off the brute's mental history." The concealment of African-American history has greatly contributed to the development of OPD-I among African Americans. A sad reality is that many African Americans whom I have encountered do not wish to know their own history. Some very ill African Americans with severe levels of OPD-I have told me that they did not want to think about slavery and the past. What these African Americans were saying to me was that they were comfortable with their illusions and did not want to disturb the delicate and precarious illusions they had created for themselves. African Americans must follow the example set by the Jews, who, as noted above, have embraced a stance that they must never forget their history and the oppression that was imposed upon them.

The Jews have created formal and informal systems of historic information transfer across generations that has been supported by society at large. African Americans, on the other hand, have been taught by their own culture and by society at large to forget and to never remember their history. For many older African Americans, for instance, discussing their life experiences with racism is painful; as a result, many refuse to discuss and to recount their life experiences with their children. To discuss their life experiences invokes not only pain but a sense of shame. The shame is born out of the fact that they permitted themselves to be treated in a less than human manner. Many older African Americans thus tend to compartmentalize and disconnect from their experiences. This disconnection with such a devastating history—and, more importantly, the disconnection with the phenomenal contributions that African Americans have made to America—keeps them in a state of dysfunction.

African Americans suffer from an identity schism. In order to rectify these practices, a strategic and culturally relevant plan that will include acknowledging the problem; teaching African-American history at home and through schools, the church, fraternal organizations, and social and civic organizations; and providing psychotherapy from practitioners who are knowledgeable about the history and the need to coach African Americans through a process of culturally relevant psychoeducation.

Steps to Recovery: Becoming Psychologically Healthy

The first step toward recovery from the impact of slavery and oppression and becoming a psychologically healthy African American is to gain an understanding and acceptance of African-American history and to understand how all African Americans are connected to it. A complete knowledge and an understanding of African-American history provides a sense of purpose and continuity that is essential for understanding who one is as an African American. African-American history forms the backdrop. Every person is defined by his or her social and cultural history. History gives meaning to the present and gives direction for the future. Without an understanding and an appreciation for history, one operates from an illusion, as Lynch stated. Many of our African-American clients have significantly altered their misguided and dysfunctional behaviors as a result of our efforts to help them identify how many of their dysfunctional behaviors derive from a lack of knowledge of their history, which should direct their sense of purpose as an African American. One book that we routinely recommend is the 1965 book *The Autobiography of Malcolm X*, a collaboration between the human-rights activist and the journalist Alex Haley, perhaps best known as the author of *Roots*. We especially recommend this book to African-American males. Malcolm X suffered from OPD-I during his early life. He was self-destructive in many ways and was eventually incarcerated as a result of his psychological dysfunction. While he was in prison, however, Malcolm X was introduced to African Amrican history by a member of the Nation of Islam. Once he embraced his history, he found his own sense of purpose and his own greatness. Armed with that knowledge, Malcolm X was transformed from a self-destructive African American to an African American of greatness.

The evidence is clear to me that knowledge of African-American history is crucial to initiating and sustaining positive behavioral change among African Americans, who must not permit "generational forgetting" to continue. The term "generational forgetting" refers to the phenomenon in which cultural events and experiences of the past are forgotten by subsequent generations. Generational forgetting is the failure of one generation to transmit to subsequent generations information relevant to their culture and experiences. For African Americans, generational forgetting is profound. By and large African Americans have little understanding of (or appreciation for) the efforts of their ancestors and the contributions they made. African Americans must not allow generational forgetting to happen. They must do as the Jews have done and never permit their history to go unknown and untold to future generations of African Americans. African Americans must pay homage to their great African-American saints, such as Saint Mary, Saint Martin, Saint Marcus, Saint Dorothy, Saint George, Saint Booker T., Saint Nathaniel, Saint Sojourner, and Saint Frederick. These are but a few of the African-American saints. I refered to them as "saints" because they understood their purpose as African Americans and gave their lives for the betterment and progress of their people. African Americans must begin to honor their contributions and find ways to honor their memory. Few, if any, memorials to these great African-American saints exist; by now there should be a memorial coin commerating Martin Luther King Jr. as a great and significant contributor to American life and culture. African Americans must not let the courage and the sacrifices of these and other great African-American saints go unknown and untold. African Americans must begin to learn and identify the saints within their own families: each and every African-American family has its own saints within the family whose contributions must be remembered and appreciated. African Americans must appreciate the sacrifices of their own immediate ancestors, grandparents, and great grandparents, simply because they endured and survived.

A Therapeutic Intervention Approach for Treating OPD-I

In September 2003 I began to devise and experiment with therapeutic intervention strategies that specifically focused on OPD-I. After twenty-five years it had become obvious to me that in order for African Americans to thrive and move toward psychological health, alternative treatment approaches needed to be researched, developed, and implemented. It was during this time in 2003 that I began to realize that African Americans by and large did not have a specific sense of purpose for their lives. I believe that a major reason for the negative acting out of African-American youth is a direct result of their starvation for a sense of relevance for their lives. By this I mean that they do not understand how they are connected to the larger scheme of things in terms of their identity as African Americans. In other words, they do not have "the big picture" or purpose for their lives. My treatment strategy thus involves using a cognitive-behavioral modification approach using African-American history as a starting point. African-American history serves as the backdrop or intervening variable. My first effort of using this therapeutic strategy was with a group of adolescents. I chose to begin with adolescents because they were accessible at the time and I believed that adolescents would be more likely to respond in a positive way. According to the literature, personality and personality disorders do not become fixed until about the age of twenty-one; adolescents thus represent the best opportunity to intervene, because their personalities are still in the process of formation. To implement this therapeutic strategy, I structured six hours—one day a week for eight weeks—as the treatment program schedule.

I chose Saturday as the day to implement this treatment approach. As a result, I began to refer to this treatment program as the "Saturday Academy." The following section will outline, with some detail, a description of the Saturday Academy treatment approach to OPD-I.

PURPOSE AND OBJECTIVES OF THE SATURDAY ACADEMY

Purpose: To help clients develop a stronger sense of purpose as African Americans and to replace the self-destructive cognitive-behavioral processes that result from OPD-I with positive and productive cognitive-behavioral processes

Objective I: To assist clients in the development of a sense of purpose as African Americans

Objective II: To create a personal identification with African-American history

Objective III: To improve academic performance and eliminate academic failure

Objective IV: To eliminate substance abuse

Objective V: To eliminate oppositional defiance

Objective VI: To eliminate conduct disorder

THE SATURDAY ACADEMY PARTICIPANTS

The participants in the first Saturday Academy consisted of ten African-American adolescents: five males and five females, ranging from fourteen to sixteen years of age. All youth were referred initially as private clients; each was screened during individual counseling sessions and agreed to participate in the Saturday Academy with the encouragement and permission of their parent(s). Each youth participant had similar presenting problems, which included conduct disorder, oppositional defiance, academic disorders (academic failure), and substance abuse. The ten youth represented various socioeconomic statuses, ranging from low income to upper-middle income.

THE SATURDAY ACADEMY FORMAT

The Saturday Academy met on eight consecutive Saturdays from ten in the morning to four in the afternoon. The assumption was that an intense immersion into the subject matter would bring about faster results in terms of producing cognitive restructuring than one-hour-a-day therapeutic sessions. The typical therapeutic format for outpatient counseling and psychotherapy is to engage a client in one to two hours of sessions per week. It has been my experience that this traditional counseling format produces very slow (if any) cognitive change. The traditional outpatient counseling format generally requires many counseling sessions to bring about the desired counseling goals. The more intense six-hour format used in the Saturday Academy produces faster and more permanent cognitive-behavioral change; this is because clients are unable to maintain their defense mechanisms for extended periods of time, and resistance by the client is thus more easily eliminated. Clients become more receptive to the therapeutic process as a result. The power of group dynamics also contributed to the therapeutic process and desired outcomes.

THE THERAPEUTIC APPROACH

The therapeutic approach involved the use of several therapeutic modalities:bibliotherapy, cinematherapy, substance abuse counseling and education, and academic tutoring and study skills. We used cinematherapy as a means of rapidly immersing the youth participants in the area of African-American history. For example, the first video we used with this group was an eight-hour video titled *Africans in America,* which traces African-American history from the introduction of Africans to America in the 1400s to the end of the Civil War in 1865; we used other videos to examine the plight of African Americans from 1865 to 1965. These videos included *Marcus Garvey, Malcolm X, Martin Luther King, The Tuskegee Airmen, 4 Little Girls, The Civil Rights Movement,* and so on. The participants watched the videos, after which we held discussions involving critical analysis. The intent of this approach was to help the participants become aware of African Americans' ongoing struggle to achieve freedom in America.

We used bibliotherapy as a means of assisting the participants in improving their reading skills while at the same time developing an appreciation for African-American history. It is my opinion that the most rapid and enduring cognitive change occurs as a result of reading. We therefore gave participants various reading assignments in the area of African-American history. Some of the books and reading assignments included *The Willie Lynch Letter, Up from Slavery, The Diary of a Slave Girl, The Autobiography of Malcolm X, Bessie Coleman, The Underground Railroad, Black Like Me, The Strange Career of Jim Crow, Narrative of Sojourner Truth, Black Rage, Narrative of the Life of Frederick Douglass, Dark Ghetto, Why Blacks Kill Blacks, The Buffalo Soldiers, George Washington Carver: Scientist and Symbol, Nat Turner,* and so on. We used the reading assignments as topics of critical discussion and analysis. We taught participants to play chess as a therapeutic tool in order to help them develop their decision-making skills. Learning chess also helped the students develop planning and implementation skills.

ACADEMIC ENRICHMENT AND TUTORING

We addressed two areas of academic functioning: reading and mathematics. The use of bibliotherapy addressed the problems associated with reading and comprehension. Participants were engaged in critical thinking and analysis of reading assignments and were also asked to write book reviews and summaries of their assigned reading materials. As a result of this approach, the youths demonstrated a significant improvement in their reading and comprehension skills. In addition to assistance with reading, the participants received mathematics tutoring and assistance. Rather than focusing on solving problems, the participants were introduced to mathematics as a language. Once they were able to "speak" the language of math, they were able to engage in problem solving and finding solutions.

In most counselling scenarios, students are typically provided with minimal problem-solving instructions and are then given a number of math problems to solve. Most often, students are provided with one or two examples of a math problem and then are given a number of math problems to solve using the examples provided. In my experience, even when students do successfully solve the math problems, they are unable to explain and articulate the process that they used to do so. At some point, students become lost; they tend to give up because they do not understand what they are doing. The Saturday Academy participants were thus introduced to math as a language.

Mathematics is actually one of two universal languages, the other one being music. The participants were taught to focus on the language of mathematics, which enabled them to explain what they were doing when they solved math problems. The participants brought their math assignments to the Saturday Academy, where we reviewed their math problems; the participants were helped so that they could explain the concepts using the language of mathematics.

Rather than focusing on problem solving, we focused on basic math concepts and formulas, and rather than concentrating on rote problem solving, we paid more attention to their ability to verbally articulate mathematical processes. Once the students were able to explain these processes using the language of mathematics, they were able to apply mathematical concepts and formulas. As a result of helping the participants to understand math as a language, the participants achieved significant improvements in their grades.

The other area of focus was substance-abuse education and counseling, which included life-skills training exercises to improve decision making and to help participants develop a more positive orientation toward life challenges. As participants progressed in the Saturday Academy, they were able to understand substance abuse as being counter to their purpose and identity as African Americans.

SATURDAY ACADEMY RESULTS

Overall, the participants in the Saturday Academy were able to develop a strong identification with their African-American history and their African-American ancestors' struggle for freedom. This understanding of African-American history was successful in helping the youth participants restructure their identities as African Americans; their self-concepts were strengthened as a result. A strong sense of purpose was imparted to each participant, each of whom left with a clear sense of personal commitment to honor his or her historical legacy. In other words, each participant was able to develop a sense of purpose beyond self and was able to understand where he or she fit in the larger scheme of things from a historical perspective.

The Saturday Academy's purpose and objectives were achieved with each youth participant; we used pre- and posttests to measure various learning objectives. The results revealed significantly increased knowledge across all areas that we measured. In addition to the youth participants' development of a positive regard for self and for other African Americans, they were able to become aware of various self-destructive behaviors and conditions that contributed to their dysfunctional cognitive-behavioral dispositions. The participants improved their academic performance; all of them have since graduated from high school. A follow-up study revealed that some of the participants have enrolled in college, and four have graduated and continue to thrive. All of the participants were successful in altering their self-destructive behaviors and now live productive lives with a sense of purpose as African Americans.

Chapter V: Toward the Next Century

More on Intervention and Treatment

With some modifications, we employed the same approach used in the Saturday Academy with our adult African-American clients. We uniformly discuss the question of purpose; the use of the Willie Lynch Letter is essential for beginning the therapeutic dialogue. Once African-American clients recognize and accept that they have been psychologically programmed to be dysfunctional, we initiate critical introspection. As a result, once they are introduced to this information and perspective, the clients begin to engage in self-analysis in an effort to identify any areas of their lives that might reflect the presence and manifestations of OPD-I. My research with African-American clients has validated the existence of the condition. African-American clients have unanimously recognized and accepted that the condition exists and have been able to identify specific behavioral expressions and thoughts that represent the condition within themselves. Therapists must recognize that African Americans have a special type of dual diagnoses: OPD-I is generally found to be a co-occurring disorder in which other behavioral and mental health issues are also present. The following list represents elements of a therapeutic approach that I have used in treating OPD-I.

A. Discuss the clients' purpose as African Americans and help them become aware of their purpose as it is defined by African-American history.

B. Help clients identify how OPD-I is being expressed in their thoughts and behaviors.

C. Help clients identify how OPD-I is manifested in their interactions with others.

D. Determine other dysfunctional behavior that may be independent of OPD-I.

E. Use cinematherapy (videos and films pertinent to African-American history).

F. Use bibliotherapy (books and publications pertinent to African-American history).

G. Utilize OPD-I support and recovery groups (it is important that African Americans share their experiences of oppression).

H. Travel to Africa, Jamaica, and other black countries and regions.

The Healthy Mind: Correcting and Undoing OPD-I

As I stated in the introduction, I have been trying to understand the uniqueness of the African-American psyche for over thirty-five years. Just as others before me, I wanted to understand the underlying motivation for the behaviors and thought processes of African Americans. As a result of this quest for understanding, I have spent the last thirty-five years studying and trying to explain the behaviors of African Americans. Based on clinical research derived from our behavioral health care facility and the contributions of other behavioral scientists and practitioners, I believe that at this point in my career I have been able to identify and give a name to the dysfunctional tendencies that are peculiar to African Americans. The OPD-I diagnosis has been able to fill this void. My quest to understand how African Americans have responded to social oppression is similar to those who seek a cure for cancer, diabetes, heart disease, and so forth. My efforts to seek a treatment for the psychoemotional damage caused by slavery and oppression has resulted in the formation of OPD-I as a diagnostic label. OPD-I as a diagnostic label captures the range of emotional and behavioral manifestations that are a result of slavery and oppression. The first step toward a cure for any disease is to establish a correct and accurate diagnosis. Once an exact diagnosis is established, a specific cure can be developed. Now that a specific diagnosis has been established, psychological healing can now begin for African Americans.

Love of Self

Another characteristic of the healthy African-American mind is to develop self-acceptance and a love for self as an African American. Many African Americans do not place any value on their blackness. Self-hatred and self-rejection are evident in the behaviors of many African Americans. One of the criterion for OPD-I is the tendency of some African Americans to emulate the behavior and characteristics of whites and white society. The psychologically unhealthy African American who exhibits OPD-I seeks to minimize any distinguishing African characteristics (hair, eyes, skin color, exaggerated and altered speech tone, etc.) in favor of Eurocentric characteristics and traits. These African Americans exhibit and express a preference for the white value system and desire to be white. While many African Americans will deny that they are attempting to be white, if one examines the behavior of some African Americans, it becomes apparent that they are at least *emulating* whites. It is necessary to state for the record that many African Americans' behavioral characteristics are unconscious or are the result of accepting certain dysfunctional behaviors as normal. Many of these behaviors can be interpreted and understood as self-rejection or a rejection of blackness.

As noted in the previous chapter, Malcolm X discussed in his autobiography this tendency of African Americans to emulate whites; he discussed the many ways that African Americans exhibit their preference for the white standard, to the extent that many African Americans attempt to appear white or as white as possible. Frantz Fanon, in his 1952 book *Black Skins, White Masks*, wrote that "the greatest desire of the black man is to be white." The clearest example of this is how African-American women and many men attempt to have "good" hair. Today you can observe many African-American women in particular wearing anything but their own hair. African-American women are making others (such as Koreans and other Asians) wealthy by buying wigs made from human and synthetic hair. Of course, many of the African-American women whom I have questioned about this trend of wearing artificial hair explain that it is "just fashion," and that it does not represent a rejection of their blackness. My response is to ask them who determines what is fashionable. Of course, whites and the white-controlled media determine what is fashionable, and African Americans accept and try to conform to these images of fashion and beauty—even though it is impossible for the average African-American woman to achieve these white-oriented images. The oddest thing to me is a "nappy-headed" blond Afro. The sad thing is that unhealthy African Americans seek to adhere to a standard they cannot possibly achieve. In Carl Rogers's terminology (1961), the healthy African-American mind is able to achieve a state of "positive self-regard" as an African American and as a person. Ultimately, psychologically healthy African Americans understand that their blackness and their personhood are not separate but are one and the same. The psychologically healthy African-American mind realizes that it does not have to conform to a standard that is alien to it. The psychologically healthy African American understands that it is appropriate to develop and establish individual standards and to develop a love and appreciation of self.

Learning to Accommodate

One characteristic or criterion for OPD-I is the manner in which many African Americans relate to one another. There is a tendency for the unhealthy African-American mind to oppress and to punish other African Americans. The healthy African-American mind that is free from OPD-I will exhibit a tendency to accommodate other African Americans whenever and wherever possible. The healthy African-American mind is one that understands that it is necessary to empower other African Americans when given the opportunity. We are all familiar with the "crab in the bucket" behavior of many psychologically unhealthy African Americans. One statement that we asked on the PDSAA is this: "I believe that black people will be fairer to white people than to other black people" (see the appendix). Of the one thousand African Americans surveyed, 70 percent stated that this statement was true. Another question we asked on the PDSAA was that "I feel that white people do more for their people than black people do for their people," 80 percent of African Americans felt was true. A similar question was that "Many of the problems that blacks face are caused by blacks," 70 percent of the African Americans who responded said was true.

These results indicate that, as a group, African Americans do not expect other African Americans to accommodate them. More significantly, these results indicate that the respondents had themselves engaged in punitive and oppressive behaviors toward other African Americans. It appears that Willie Lynch was successful in creating discord among the slaves, and this divisiveness can still be observed in the behavior of African Americans who have severe levels of OPD-I. Lynch stated that "I use fear, distrust, and envy for control purposes." The healthy African-American mind, realizing that African Americans have to empower one another, will learn to assist and accommodate other African Americans. When people are powerless, they will tend to oppress one another. I experienced this tendency for African Americans to oppress other African Americans the morning I wrote this section. I had to go to the municipal court building to pay a traffic fine; African Americans were in charge of security and managed the cashier's office. My encounter with these African Americans was disappointing, to say the least. The security officer barked her instructions to me as if I were an undesirable person. The African-American woman at the cashier's office was equally hostile in her attitude toward me, and she began dictating what I needed to do and what the negative consequences would be if I didn't comply with her orders. These hostile and oppressive attitudes are a daily occurrence when dealing with other African Americans, and these behaviors indicate the presence of OPD-I.

Another example of the unhealthy African-American mind is the tendency to minimize and undermine other African Americans. This unhealthy behavioral tendency can be observed at many different levels. If you happened to see the movie *Barbershop*, for example, then you will remember Cedric the Entertainer when he made pejorative, belittling statements about Martin Luther King Jr. and Rosa Parks. These statements about Dr. King and Mrs. Parks were minimizing and reflected a severe level of OPD-I in that character. The unhealthy African-American mind is akin to the behaviors of a spoiled and overindulged child. The unhealthy African American suffering from OPD-I will exhibit ignorance, disrespect, and ungrateful attitudes about the contributions of other significant African Americans.

Other races and ethnicities pay homage to their ancestors; they seek every opportunity to show their gratitude toward their leaders, both past and present. They will create and erect memorials of every form to help them remember and honor the contributions of their people. The Jews engage in the same kind of behavior when remembering those who were lost in the Holocaust. This is why you will find many Holocaust museums and related efforts to pay homage to their ancestors. African Americans must begin to engage in open acknowledgment of the many African Americans who have contributed to the struggle for freedom. I would like to see more monuments, sculptures, and other memorials that would celebrate the accomplishments of great African Americans. Where can you take your child to see the busts and figures of great African Americans? The psychologically healthy African American will understand the need to honor and not minimize the contributions of great African Americans. The healthy African-American mind will also understand the need to respect the efforts of other African Americans who are contributing to the collective good of all African Americans. In conclusion, psychologically healthy African Americans will accommodate rather than punish other African Americans. They will not exhibit a negative and hostile attitude toward other African Americans; rather, they will present a positive and helpful attitude when encountering other African Americans.

At this point I must provide a few examples of what I mean by "accommodating" other African Americans. About two years ago, our agency was late in paying the electric bill. The payment was two months behind because of the slow payment of a few government contracts that the agency had at the time. In the middle of a typical Friday, a thirtysomething African-American male from the electric company arrived to disconnect our electricity because of late payment. I began to plead with him to not disconnect the electricity. I informed him that I could make the payment while he was there in order to prove my sincerity. He stated that there was nothing that he could do because the order to disconnect had already been placed; he was simply doing his job. I continued to plead with him and asked if he could do something to help without jeopardizing his job; I understood that he was simply doing his job and following his company's orders. The young man apologized and went outside to the rear of the property, where the electric meter was located. So I waited for the electricity to go off. About five minutes later, the young man returned and stated that he could not get to the meter because a tree was in the way and that he would have to come back on Monday. This young man decided to use his discretion in the matter, and as a result he accommodated both me and the facility. This is what I mean by accommodating one another when we can and have the power to do so. If this young African-American man had not accommodated me in my request, the agency would have had to spend an additional $700 to have the electricity turned back on. This was $700 that remained in the African-American community instead of in the pockets of the electric company. This young man later told me that a business in the same area as ours owed more than $9,000 and that their electricity had not been scheduled for disconnection. Healthy African-American minds understand that by accommodating one another, they are strengthening their community and that they are a part of that community. The unhealthy African-American mind, in contrast, fails to see the connection and tends to think individualistically and punitively toward other African Americans.

I have to give another similar example as the one I've just provided. Approximately one year later, our agency again failed to pay the electric bill on time. Again a young, thirtysomething African-American male came to disconnect the electricity. I again pleaded as I had before. This young African-American "brother," however, wasn't hearing it. I told him that I could pay right then. I asked him to use his personal power to accommodate our agency and explained why he should help if he could. I soon saw that the more I pleaded with him, the more he was determined to exercise his discretion in the negative. In other words, he seemed to take pleasure in demonstrating his power over me in this situation. He was affirming himself and his own need for personal power by disconnecting the electricity. Well, I paid the past-due bill and the additional deposit and a priority reconnect fee. Naturally, I assumed that when I arrived the next day, the electricity would be restored. To my surprise, the electricity was not on, although I had paid the eighty-dollar priority reconnecting fee. When I phoned the electric company, I learned that this "brother" had also removed the electric meter altogether; the company stated that the building required a "three-phase" electric meter. To make a long story short, this mentally unhealthy young African-American man had gone a step further and punished us by removing the electric meter entirely. He actually went out of his way to inconvenience the agency in conducting its business. He was being vindictive in his actions toward both me and the agency. It took the entire day to have the meter replaced. This same young man was supposed to return to reconnect the meter, but he gave the job to another worker, who happened to be white. When I asked about the other "black" man who was supposed to reconnect the meter, the new worker told me that his coworker did not want to service us and had asked him if they could trade jobs and if he could reinstall the meter himself. Perhaps you have experienced similar circumstances where another African American refused to accommodate you when he or she had the power to do so. I have had numerous examples in my own life experiences where African Americans were more considerate of whites than of their fellow African Americans. I am sure you have had similar experiences if you are an African American.

Another example I must provide of the unhealthy African-American mind in action involves an incident that occurred in my life about a year before I wrote this. I was selling a small rental house that I owned and had to order an appraisal. The buyer was another African-American male who considered himself a real estate investor. At the time, I was offering the house at about $12,000 less than the market value because I wanted a quick sale. Well, this African-American real estate investor made an offer for the asking price, but he wanted me to sign a contract for another $12,000 beyond my asking price. He assured me that he was going to use the additional money to update the home; he also stated that he had a friend who would appraise the house at a level that would accommodate his higher mortgage-loan request. To make another long story short, the appraisal was $5,000 less than what the buyer anticipated, and therefore he had signed a contract for $5,000 more than the appraised marked value. Of course, he asked me to forgive the $5,000 and to assume his tax liability for the additional amount above my asking price. Needless to say, the deal was off.

It turned out this man was trying to be "slick" and take advantage of my goodwill. I released him from the contract, which I could have enforced by filing a lawsuit. Instead, I placed the house back on the market. Remember, the house had already been appraised. When a new buyer applied for a mortgage loan, however, another appraisal was needed that would name the new mortgage company. I gave the name of the appraiser to the mortgage company so that they could order a copy of the appraisal. In most cases, a copy of an appraisal will generally cost about one-half of what the original appraisal cost. In this case, the copy of the appraisal should have cost anywhere between $100 to $150 at most. As is typical with the unhealthy African-American mind, this African-American real-estate appraiser would not return the mortgage company's calls or e-mails, which then called me to see if I could obtain a copy of the appraisal on their behalf. The expense of the appraisal copy was an expense to me as the seller of the property. When I did contact the appraiser, he wanted another $350 for an appraisal he had already performed. The reason he did not return the mortgage company's calls and e-mails was because he would not demand $350 from them, because he knew that they expected to pay less for a copy of an existing appraisal. So what he did was to extort more money from me, a fellow African American, but he would not try to exploit a white-owned company.

This is another example of how the unhealthy African-American mind will not accommodate fellow African Americans. As a result of his actions, he lost six other appraisal jobs I could have referred to him. I could go on with example after example of how African Americans will refuse to accommodate one another. But the healthy African-American mind understands and appreciates the need to be accommodating toward other African Americans when there is no reason not to be.

Self-Sufficiency

At this juncture in the war for independence, freedom, and liberty, African Americans are like adolescents. African Americans have the ability and the potential to become self-governing and economically independent if they are willing to unite for the common benefit of the entire community. I believe the next achievement for African Americans is to become economically self-sufficient. Like adolescents, African Americans have the mind to be independent and they insist on being treated as such, but the reality is that African Americans are still economically dependent on whites. Until African Americans own their own banks and other financial institutions, they will remain economically dependent. There is a great need for financial education within the African-American community. Most African Americans do not understand how money works or what it takes to become financially independent. This is why you can observe the proliferation of pawnshops and payday loan stores in the African-American community. It is further evidence of continued economic exploitation of African Americans. The presence of these predatory financial businesses is symptomatic of the fact that African Americans suffer from a lack of financial acumen. In other words, the payday loan stores and pawnshops within the African-American community indicate that African Americans are suffering financially. The healthy African-American mind understands that money equals power and that without money one is powerless. The Nation of Islam appears to understand the need for financial independence: they encourage all of their followers to work toward financial independence as individuals and to work toward economic self-sufficiency as a community. African Americans with healthy minds understand the relationship between freedom and economic independence. All African Americans, no matter their socioeconomic status, can begin to improve their finances by taking small steps such as saving their change and establishing a financial plan.

Another statement that we asked on the PSDAA questionnaire was: "I feel that white people will always be in charge." Approximately 30 percent of African Americans stated that this was true. A significant number of African Americans—almost a third—therefore believe that whites will always rule them, and therefore they will not attempt to work toward independence and self-sufficiency. Along these same lines, the following statement was included on the PSDAA: "Black people have the power to overcome discrimination." The encouraging news is that 70 percent of African Americans believed this statement to be true. While the Million Man March of 1995 was a great show of support by the African-American community, economically speaking, the African-American community was the big loser. When I think about all the money that was spent on travel, food, hotels, and so on, I know that collectively, African Americans spent several million dollars to attend the event, but it was mostly nonblack business owners who benefited economically.

I heard from those who attended that they heard wonderful speeches and that they felt a great sense of renewal from participating. I asked an acquaintance who had attended the march if anyone had "passed the hat." He asked me what I meant by that. I responded that if a million African-American men were in attendance, then someone should have passed a hat and collected one dollar for each man in attendance to start a bank; if each man had committed just one dollar per month for the next twelve months, then a total of $13,000,000 could have been easily raised. This money could have been used to start a bank, or it could have been deposited into one of the existing African-American banks. The healthy African-American mind seeks to become self-sufficient economically and not remain dependent economically. Healthy African-American minds are aware where and how their dollars are spent and will seek to do business within their community first. Yet many African Americans seek to impress others by spending big money with other races instead of their own. Because of the presence of OPD-I, many African Americans seek affirmation from whites by patronizing their businesses.

Another dysfunctional trend among African Americans is to be dependent on the welfare system. It is common knowledge that African Americans are disproportionately dependent on the welfare system. As I briefly touched on earlier, many African Americans represent the third generation of welfare dependency. I am referring to those African Americans who use the welfare system to sustain themselves and not to those who have received assistance because of a special need or circumstance. I am referring to those African Americans who have made welfare an intergenerational lifestyle. Unhealthy African Americans who suffer from severe OPD-I believe that they are "getting over" on the system. In their dysfunctional state of mind, they do not realize that they are selling out their own lives. These intergenerational welfare recipients have come to accept their dependency; as a result, they have lost all personal pride and lack the motivation to become self-sufficient.

Affirmation

In an effort to seek affirmation from whites, the unhealthy African-American mentality will cause those who suffer from OPD-I to act as collaborators in their own oppression. In other words, many African Americans act as agents of oppression by implementing and carrying out the oppressive agendas of their companies and/or employers, who are primarily white. The oppressors of African Americans have learned to use African Americans to do their dirty work against other African Americans. By employing African Americans to carry out their oppressive agendas against African Americans, they seek to utilize other African Americans in order to avoid the appearance of discrimination and racism. By using African Americans against other African Americans, they can say it was an African American who carried out the act and therefore it could not have been discrimination. Some behaviors or actions when acted out by whites can be interpreted as racism, but when the same act is implemented by an African American, it can be explained as conducting regular business within the normal course of doing business. For example, say an African American worker files a lawsuit alleging racism and discrimination against her white supervisor; in an effort to exonerate himself, the white defendant will engage an African American to defend him. This is a kind of reverse psychology to hide acts of discrimination and racism. The sad fact is that too many African Americans are willing to act as collaborators in such ploys in the name of professionalism. Most often in these circumstances, however, these collaborating African Americans seek acceptance and affirmation by whites. The healthy African-American mind does not seek affirmation from whites as a basis for establishing self-worth. The healthy African-American mind will not voluntarily engage in collaboration against other African Americans.

The Twenty-First-Century African-American Mentality

The list below summarizes the psychological transformations that are necessary for African Americans to begin healing themselves. African Americans must make a cognitive shift that will reflect the kind of thoughts and behaviors that will lead them toward psychological health and emotional well-being.

THE NEW AFRICAN AMERICAN MENTALITY VS. THE OLD AFRICAN-AMERICAN MENTALITY

Empowerment Thinking vs. Survival Thinking

Collective Efforts vs. Individual Efforts

Recognition vs. Denial

Trust vs. Distrust

Loyalty vs. Disloyalty

Unification vs. Division

Rehabilitation vs. Abandonment

Self-Love vs. Self-Hate

Personal Responsibility vs. Dependence and Avoidance

Faith vs. Fear

Appreciation vs. Envy

Economic Responsibility vs. Economic Irresponsibility

African Americans must begin the journey toward achieving a healthy mind, which will lead to a total sense of well-being. This journey toward psychological health will require a conscious effort to develop a new empowerment thought process. I have outlined below several steps that will help to reverse the dysfunctional psychological programming that has occurred among African Americans:

1. Learn and develop an intimate understanding of African-American history.

2. Understand your purpose as an African American: to continue the struggle for freedom and economic power.

3. Accommodate other African Americans whenever and wherever you can; stop punishing and oppressing other African Americans.

4. Discontinue minimizing other African Americans: give credit where credit is due. Honor your ancestors and remember their sacrifices.

5. Work collectively with other African Americans.

6. Seek professional counseling for individual and family problems.

7. Stop imitating white people and learn to appreciate the unique African-American self.

8. Be productive rather than destructive.

9. Heed Booker T. Washington's advice and "save your money, buy land, and learn a skill."

10. Develop rather than abandon African-American neighborhoods.

11. Have your DNA analyzed to learn your African origin and heritage.

Chapter VI: The New Imperative for African Americans

Come On, People

When I began to write this manuscript, Dr. Bill Cosby was not yet embroiled in the controversy that currently confronts him. I am referring to the accusations by women who over thirty years later have accused him of inappropriate behavior. Dr. Cosby does not need any defense of his comments, statements, and observations of the issues that the African-American community faces. In their 2007 book *Come On, People: On the Path from Victims to Victors*, Dr. Cosby and his coauthor, the aforementioned Dr. Alvin Poussaint, offered an imperative for the African-American community. They stated that it was time for African Americans to assume responsibility for correcting the many issues that confront them and to stop blaming white people for many of the problems that can only be corrected by African Americans themselves. The fact is that many African Americans are ignorant, disrespectful, destructive, and irresponsible, and they themselves create much of the chaos that can be found in African-American communities.

The doctors have asserted that many of the problems the African-American community faces have to be addressed from within the community; white people are not directly responsible for many of the dysfunctional behaviors that exist for African Americans. For example, it is blacks who are killing blacks; it is blacks who are selling drugs to other blacks; it is African Americans who have the highest high-school dropout rates; it is African Americans who are disproportionately incarcerated; it is African Americans who currently have the highest incidence of AIDS; it is largely African Americans who still live in housing projects; it is African Americans who lead the way in teen pregnancies; it is African Americans who have the highest unemployment rates; and the list goes on. Are they wrong about these facts and that African Americans alone have the power and the responsibility to correct these deficiencies? It is not the white community's responsibility to address internal issues for African Americans. I agree with Drs. Cosby and Poussaint that it is time for African Americans to begin looking inwardly to solve many of the problems they face in society.

In order for African Americans to progress, they must address the many internal problems they all know exist within their community. In their book, Drs. Cosby and Poussaint discuss many of the areas of concern within the African-American community. They make an appeal to African Americans to begin empowering themselves by taking action and taking control of their communities; instead of blaming whites for all their issues, they urge African Americans to assume greater personal responsibility. Some African Americans will say that many of the internal issues within the African-American community are a result of ongoing racism. Although I would agree that racism is alive and well and can still be felt and witnessed in many arenas, I also believe that African Americans do have a choice in how they respond to oppression and racism. While many of these issues have resulted from slavery and oppression, it still remains the work of African Americans to correct these destructive behaviors. African Americans have the responsibility to help and assist those who have become dysfunctional and destructive in their efforts to cope. In other words, instead of criticizing those who are making an effort to help, those who are aware and have the ability to assist must begin to consciously do so. A new era of consciousness must be had in order for African Americans to emerge and to push forward to their higher calling, but it will be difficult for African Americans to remedy these ongoing issues within the African-American community until they understand the psychological programming that has resulted in the development of the personality disorder I refer to as OPD-I. First, because people won't seek a remedy or a cure unless they are aware that they are ill, understanding and recognizing the existence of OPD-I is an essential first step toward attaining psychological health. Otherwise, people will not seek a cure; they will only continue to manifest the symptoms of the illness.

African Americans fight individual, organizational, social, and cultural forces on a daily basis that continue to oppress and suppress their functioning at all levels. African Americans in the United States thus face a constant psychological, emotional, social, and cultural rift. For example, African Americans struggle to reconcile the concept of "We the people" under the Constitution as those who are ostensibly entitled to all the rights and privileges of citizenship. Despite their best efforts, most African Americans fail to achieve a sense of psychological wholeness and emotional health because the powers that be work relentlessly to ensure that they will not attain well-being or a wholesome and integrated sense of self. The idea of full citizenship and equal educational, political, and economic access for African Americans is untenable to the white power structure. This type of change would no doubt completely upset the order that whites have come to take for granted.

While African Americans desire external forces to somehow change in order to embrace them, they fail to understand that this will probably not happen. African Americans have little to no control over these domains, so they are fighting a losing battle; this results in mental anguish, psychological dysfunction, and cognitive dissonance. Grier and Cobbs noted in their 1968 book *Black Rage* (mentioned earlier) that "Negroes want to change inside but find it difficult to do so unless things outside are changed as well." The authors further state that "it is clear that the simplistic solution of 'more education' is meaningless when a society is more attuned to race than it is to academic achievement." Witness the stark reality reflected in the disproportionate pay schedule for African Americans who achieve higher educational attainment than their white counterparts yet continue to receive lower pay for the same jobs. There is no justice here and certainly no justifiable explanation for the difference when education and training are accounted for. The only realistic and healthy solution for African Americans is for them to recognize that they must embrace change where they do have control. Specifically, African Americans must become introspective and turn within to modify their psychological orientation in such a manner that they can begin to heal themselves both psychologically and emotionally. In 1919 the NAACP, through its Program for Change, called for basic rights for blacks. The group also noted that "this fight for rights is the Negro's fight. Who would be free, himself must strike the blow."

I say today that if a healing change is to come, it will rest largely within the African-American community. This does not in any way excuse whites from their role in also fighting this fight, for it is white society that has put laws, ordinances, and now social customs in place to maintain the convention of the exclusion of African Americans from having full access to the resources of American society. While African Americans must fight via organizations such as the NAACP and the courts to bring about fair and equitable access to resources, African Americans must also rise to the challenge of doing all they can to be fully competitive within American society. Changes at the institutional level will be slow in coming, but African Americans can take charge and make an immediate impact at their own personal level, within their families, and in their communities. African Americans must start with themselves as individuals. Clinically speaking, African Americans will not become psychologically healthy until they first recognize that a large part of their dysfunction is grounded in the historical fact of slavery and the residual effects that slavery has had and continues to have on their daily lives. Acknowledging this fact in no way relieves African Americans of their obligation to confront the psychological bondage and residual effects of this reality. What it does do is put them in the driver's seat by giving the malfunction a name and developing an understanding of the nature of their challenge. African Americans have struggled to make sense out of something that cannot make sense—as long as they allow others to cripple them with a misguided diagnosis. It is my premise, however, that African Americans, across the board, suffer from a disproportionate level of personality dysfunction. Thus, the dysfunctions manifested in African Americans today are the direct effect and result of slavery and oppression through intergenerational psychosocial transmission. The mental and physical health issues that African Americans experience have their roots in the attendant residual effects of slavery and oppression. Based on the best science, it is generally understood that a symbiotic relationship may be found among one's mental, physical, emotional, and spiritual being. As a result, the effective treatment of African Americans depends on correctly defining and labeling their condition. It is thus imperative that an appropriate diagnosis that would consider the phenomenological context of African Americans be established.

Whatever Happened to Black Psychology?

African-American clinicians have a unique responsibility to address the multitude of mental-health concerns that exist within the African-American community. African-American mental-health professionals require a new imperative. R. V. Guthrie (1980) states that "due to the urgency of our mission, black psychology should not only attempt to understand behavior, it should disseminate its scientific findings directly to the community as soon as possible, in a manner that lends itself to application." Unfortunately, the vast majority of African Americans who have been educated and trained in the field of behavioral sciences and behavioral health are employed and work outside the African-American community. Many work for predominately white-owned and white-managed agencies, universities, school districts, public agencies, and so on. The vast majority of African-American psychologists are employed at predominately white universities, where they work feverishly to obtain tenure. I often jokingly say that African-American psychologists are working very hard to guarantee themselves a permanent place on the plantation. While there is nothing wrong with African-American behavioral-health professionals working in predominately white agencies and institutions, I do believe that African-American behavioral-health professionals should be working at least on a part-time basis in the African-American community, where they are needed most.

I have had the experience of working in predominately white agencies and institutions. The fact is that the agenda and the mission of white-owned and white-managed institutions do not address the needs of the African-American community. Another observation I have made is that when African-American behavioral professionals do establish a private practice, it is generally in the white part of town or in areas they consider to be upwardly mobile. I am reminded of a tenet of the great Booker T. Washington, who stated in his 1895 "Atlanta Compromise" speech, "lower your bucket where you are" (Harland 1974). Both George Washington Carver and Booker T. Washington turned down many offers from whites who sought their employment. Even the famous industrialist Henry Ford could not persuade Dr. Carver to leave Tuskegee University. Drs. Washington and Carver understood their need to share themselves with their own community—the people who needed them most. As a result of their dedication, both men are represented in history as great men: two black saints. Today, however, African-American behavioral-health professionals seek to become part of the white mainstream.

Few African-American behavioral-health professionals appear to understand that the behavioral-health-care industry is a multibillion-dollar-a-year business. African-American behavioral-health professionals need to understand that there is plenty of money to be made in the African-American community providing mental health, substance abuse, and other related services. Since 1983 I have had at least a part-time private practice within the African-American community while I was employed by other agencies and while working in a university. In 1994 I decided to enter private practice full time. By 1999 I had to expand my private practice into a facility-level operation because I could not meet the growing demand for services. In addition to private insurance clients, my facility has a number of contracts with the city, the county, and the state. I have never had to advertise our services. I actually made a decision not to advertise, because the demand would exceed our ability to meet the demand. A great deal of planning has to be done to accommodate an ever-increasing demand.

One problem with agency and facility expansion is the fact that African-American and Hispanic behavioral-health professionals are unavailable for employment, because they are employed outside of their communities. African-American behavioral-health professionals are missing out on the tremendous financial opportunities that exist within their own community. Because the university-level education and training of behavioral-health professionals do not include the business aspects of the field, the big money in behavioral health care is made by businesspeople who are not trained in the field. As I noted above, the African-American community has a tremendous need for behavioral health-care services. While African-American behavioral health-care professionals can make a lot of money servicing that community, they must first recognize how OPD-I is being manifested within themselves. They have to first heal themselves psychologically before they will be able to effectively begin to assist African-American clients in resolving the lingering effects of oppression. I hesitate to use the following description of African-American behavioral-health professionals, but as I see it they have sold out to the establishment. Black psychology has been traded in like a used car for multiculturalism and diversity. It is time for African-American behavioral-health professionals to return to their own community and to help assist in the healing process of the African-American community—beginning with themselves.

On Reparations

Another imperative is the continued fight for reparations for African Americans. I do not pretend to be an expert on reparations; other African Americans have been fighting this war to address this issue for some time now. There is no doubt that African Americans are due some form of compensation from the United States as other groups in the nation have obtained, such as Japanese Americans and Native Americans. It was African Americans who built and defended America over a span of centuries, yet African Americans have been denied their rightful rewards for the tremendous sacrifices they have been forced to endure. Compensation has been provided to every other group that has suffered any form of undue hardship in the United States. Congressperson John Conyers, through his bill H. R. 40, proposes that Congress create a commission to study the effects of slavery upon African Americans. Conyers proposes that the bill will do four things:

1. The bill will acknowledge the fundamental injustice and inhumanity of slavery.

2. The bill will establish a commission to study slavery and its subsequent racial and economic discrimination against freed slaves.

3. The bill will study the impact of those forces on today's living African Americans.

4. The bill, by its very adoption, will authenticate the plight that African Americans have suffered at the hands of slavery.

This action could go a long way toward the healing process of helping African Americans achieve wholeness. External acknowledgment can help promote psychosocial healing. Gaining recognition that some of the dysfunctional behavior of African Americans is based, at least in part, in the institution of slavery and subsequent systemic practices of discrimination can give power to promote self-healing.

In following the reparations movement I have found that two areas appear to create stumbling blocks. The first area of controversy involves the argument that slavery occurred too many years ago to be relevant today, that African Americans today are not the ones who suffered or should be compensated, and that not all white Americans participated in slavery and oppression. My response to this argument is threefold. First of all, African Americans have had freedom under the law for only fifty years, with the CRA of 1964. Many living African Americans—including myself—have thus experienced legalized oppression firsthand. While some white Americans have not or did not directly participate in slavery and oppression, they most certainly did not openly oppose it; furthermore, all white Americans have benefited from the enslavement and oppression of African Americans either directly or indirectly. While slavery officially ended in 1865, the lingering effects of slavery and continued legalized oppression are very much evident in the suffering of African Americans today, as evidenced by the existence of OPD-I. The condition essentially amounts to a kind of disability experienced by African Americans of today as a direct result of slavery and legalized oppression.

The second area of controversy involving reparations involves the way in which African Americans should be compensated. Many people have proposed solutions, but none seem to satisfy all concerned. I have given much thought to this dilemma, and I would like to offer what I consider to be a win-win solution. The solution proposed by this author is that *for the next two hundred fifty years, African Americans are relieved from paying any form of taxes, especially federal income taxes, and that college education is provided to all African Americans who seek it without cost to them.*

With this solution, the federal government does not have to come up with immediate cash, and the omission of tax payments would assist each and every working African-American family to have more money at their disposal to help close the wealth gap. To me this is a simple and fair solution, since African Americans have been paying federal income taxes for generations without the same freedom and the benefits provided to white Americans. In other words, Africans Americans were denied their rights under the law while simultaneously being made to pay taxes. How unfair has America been toward the African American? I believe that until America comes to terms with the exploitation of African Americans and makes reparations, it will never be the great nation it could be.

Chapter VII: New Directions

As a result of hundreds of years of exclusion from the economic mainstream, African Americans have not developed their understanding of how to function in a free-market economy; African Americans have therefore been confined to competing among themselves. This within-group competitiveness has created an unnatural state of affairs in the African-American community in which African Americans are in constant conflict with one another at all levels of interaction. This conflict, which is visible at both the interpersonal and community levels, has resulted in African Americans' collective inability to cooperate. Willie Lynch's proposed use of fear, envy, and distrust to divide African Americans was largely successful. As a result, much of what African Americans deal with on a daily basis is interpersonal drama and conflict when they could be focusing on economic independence and self-reliance. Money represents power in American society, and without money one is powerless. I do not believe that African Americans understand that money represents abstract power. It appears that many African Americans view money only as a means of personal consumption, which explains why African Americans are willing to readily exchange their money for material possessions and general consumption. As a result of this consumption orientation, African Americans as a group remain economically powerless; because of this powerlessness, and because they cannot exercise power on a larger scale, African Americans tend to seek power in dysfunctional ways by attempting to control one another.

This powerlessness on a larger scale leaves only the exercise of power at the interpersonal level. In other words, African Americans appear to be largely engaged in interpersonal struggles in order to gain a sense of personal power. During my thirty-five years of counseling and research, I have concluded that 90 percent of what African Americans deal with on a daily basis involves their personal drama. When one is consumed by personal drama and conflict, one cannot effectively engage in achievement-oriented behavior and cannot work with others. African Americans must first address the solution at the personal level by understanding and recognizing the existence of OPD-I among themselves; once they achieve an understanding of OPD-I, they can then make changes at the personal level. African Americans can devise solutions to many of the dilemmas they face at both the individual and collective levels.

In order to convey the meaning and essence of what African Americans need to do to begin their journey toward psychological healing and health, I will offer a story, or parable, about a bear in the woods.

THE BEAR IN THE WOODS

Once upon a time there was a man who was visiting a strange country. He wanted to explore the beautiful forest and the countryside, so one day he went out alone, wandering the countryside to learn more about this strange but wonderful country. The man became so fascinated by the forest that he lost track of time; soon nightfall was upon him. He began to try to find his way out of the forest. As he walked and wandered, he became more lost as he wandered deeper into the forest; he lost his bearings and became hopelessly lost. He decided to find a comfortable and safe spot to sleep for the night before trying to find his way out of the forest at first daylight.

As daylight dawned the next morning, he rose and began to look for a way out of the forest. He wandered all day and ended up deeper in the forest and more lost than before. He was unable to find his way out of the forest. So again he had to spend another night in the forest, cold, scared, and alone.

For the next several days, the man was still unable to find his way home. One day led to the next, and he eventually came to understand that he may be lost in this forest forever. Day after day he would try in vain to find his way. It became difficult for him to survive. He had to search for food constantly; to make matters worse, a huge bear had gotten his scent and was tracking him all the time. The man not only had to try to find food and shelter, but he had to avoid being eaten by the huge bear. As time passed the man began to grow weary and dispirited. He felt like giving up. The bear almost caught him on numerous occasions.

One day the man saw the big bear go up a nearby mountain. The man decided to go to the river to get a drink of water and catch a fish. He knew that he had to hurry, because the bear would soon return to the river to catch fish and drink water. As the man washed his face in the river, he looked up and saw another man on the riverbank across from him. At first he could not believe his eyes: he thought he was hallucinating, because he had not seen another human in such a long time. As he rubbed his eyes to clear his vision, he was sure that another person was standing just on the other side of the river. The man waved, and the other man waved back. The man was delighted that he was no longer alone in the woods, so he crossed the river to greet the other man. They were happy to see each other. They began to speak to each other, and they both shared their stories about how they had become lost in the woods. They were overjoyed that they were no longer alone.

As they discussed their mutual plight, the first man asked the other if he knew about the big bear. This man had also been avoiding being captured and eaten by the big bear. They decided to work together in order to make it easier to survive. They even made a plan to trap and kill the bear, because the bear threatened them both. They shook hands and agreed to work together for mutual survival. As the two men visited with each other, they began to share their experiences and backgrounds. It turned out that the two men were very different in many ways. One man was a Christian and the other a Muslim; one was a Republican and the other a Democrat; one was a Blood and the other a Crip; one was educated and the other was not; one came from the south side, the other from the north side. The more they talked, the more differences they discovered. Soon they began to doubt that they could really work together because of their many differences; they eventually decided that they could not work together after all.

The two men went their separate ways. On that same evening, one of the men was captured and eaten by the big bear. The big bear was pleased and had himself a good Christian meal of the first man. Then the big bear decided to begin searching for the other man. A few days later the big bear was able to catch the other man, and this time had himself a good Muslim meal. The bear was fat and happy after feasting on the two men. The bear wondered if there were others like them who were lost in his forest.

***

The story ends here. Both men were eventually eaten by the big bear because they could not work together. You see, the big bear did not care about their differences; he just wanted some meat to eat. The big bear did not care what their religion was, he did not care what gang they belonged to, he did not care about what side of town they came from; the bear just wanted some meat. Both men perished because they let their differences keep them from working together for mutual survival. The story I just told has another ending. In this ending the two men decided to put their differences aside and work together because it would be easier for both of them to survive by doing so. They realized that by working together they stood a better chance. They made a plan to trap and kill the big bear, because he was the main threat to their survival. After doing a little planning, the two men devised a trap and were able to kill the big bear. They celebrated their victory over the bear. They now had fur coats to keep them warm; they had bear ribs and steaks to eat; they had bear oil to use; they used the bear's bones to make weapons for self-defense and hunting. The two men were now living well because they came together and destroyed the big bear that was threatening them both.

It is time for African Americans to psychologically restore themselves to their natural state of being and to continue their long journey toward autonomy and independence, but having autonomy and independence means becoming economically self-sufficient instead of being economically dependent. African Americans' ancestors have already accomplished much of the difficult work. Today, however, the task that lies just ahead may be the most difficult; that task is to engage in self-examination and self-correction in order to overcome the horrible psychological effects of slavery and oppression that have resulted in OPD-I. African Americans must regain and reacquire the humanity that has been compromised and lost over centuries of oppression. African Americans must recapture their full humanity that was lost and taken from them. The external barriers to freedom and liberty have been removed. African Americans must remember that those who would deny and disregard their rights continue to work at their program of oppression. African Americans must understand the nature of systemic oppression as it exists today: substandard education, economic discrimination, a biased criminal justice system, overdependence on the welfare system, the spread of HIV/AIDS and moral decay, the selling of illegal and legal drugs to African Americans, and so forth.

Up to this moment, someone else has been in control of the lives and destiny of African Americans. It is now up to African Americans to determine what their future will be. Either African Americans will continue down a self-destructive path as their oppressors have intended or they will recognize the reality of their purpose and destiny and will rise to the challenge that lies before them. The solution lies within each and every African American. One by one, African Americans have to correct themselves and begin their personal journey to recover their authentic selves and to eliminate the satanic effects of slavery and oppression. African Americans must learn from the two men in the story above and put aside their differences and begin working together for mutual survival. In his 1900 book *A New Negro for a New Century*, Booker T. Washington discussed the changes necessary for the relatively recently freed slaves to begin their journey as free people. His solution is still viable for the African American in the new millennium. He stated that Negros (African Americans) should acquire education, learn skills, buy land, and save their money. His solution remains a sound approach in the twenty-first century. I would only add that African Americans have to begin working collectively in order to achieve their personal and collective goals.

It has been my goal to describe some of the ways in which African Americans have become dysfunctional, and I have given the dysfunction a name that represents a mental health diagnosis. I have also tried to offer some direction for devising a solution and treatment perspective to address the problem. It will be up to others in the behavioral health-care field to authenticate or, in academic terms, to validate the existence of OPD-I. My research and clinical experiences are limited and will, without a doubt, be attacked. Indeed, I fully expect that people will strive to discredit my findings and observations. Nevertheless, the truth is self-evident. It is my hope that further discussion, examination, and research will ignite a new and long-overdue movement that will catapult African Americans a bit closer to the mountaintop that Dr. Martin Luther King Jr. alluded to. African Americans have been forced into and kept in the darkness for over half a millennium now. Willie Lynch was correct in his assertion that "the mind has a strong drive to correct and to recorrect itself over a period of time"; that time is now for African Americans to begin correcting and recorrecting their minds. As Lynch stated, this recorrecting of the mind has to begin with African Americans learning their history; only then can they expect to gain the proper perspective for the corrective thought process to begin.

African Americans cannot expect others to teach them their great and proud history; they will have to do it for themselves. African Americans must turn off the TV, radio, video games, phones, and the many other distractions that are designed to keep them entertained and ignorant. They must teach themselves and their children and make it a life priority to continue that learning and teaching. African Americans can begin utilizing the organizations and institutions in their communities, such as the church, private schools, book clubs, historically black colleges and universities, fraternities and sororities, and fraternal and other community organizations. Just as the Jews have vowed to never forget their treatment, African Americans must embrace what has been referred to as the "black holocaust" and never forget their holy struggle for freedom and dignity and the many great achievements of African Americans, past and present. There is much to be proud of in spite of the tremendous difficulties African Americans have faced in America, and African Americans must learn and begin to appreciate these accomplishments as they learn to love and to value themselves. May God continue to be with African Americans today, as he has been in their past.

Appendix: Psychosocial Development Scale for African Americans (PDSAA)

Respondents are asked to answer each of the following questions by circling T for True or F for False.

T/F 1. I feel it is necessary to know black history.

T/F 2. I feel that only God can solve some of my problems.

T/F 3. I feel that most white people are smarter than most black people.

T/F 4. I sometimes worry about fitting in with white people.

T/F 5. Most white people I know care about me.

T/F 6. I feel that I would be more successful if I were white.

T/F 7. I have never experienced racial discrimination.

T/F 8. It is better to try to get along with whites.

T/F 9. I prefer to live and work with only black people.

T/F 10. I have some white friends.

T/F 11. I feel that there is no difference between black and white people.

T/F 12. I feel that black people are as good as white people.

T/F 13. Some people I know don't like white people.

T/F 14. White people are responsible for racism.

T/F 15. I believe that black people will help other blacks if they can.

T/F 16. I believe that black people will be fairer to white people than to other black people.

T/F 17. I believe that black people hate themselves.

T/F 18. To speak like white people will make you sound more intelligent.

T/F 19. To speak like white people will make you blend in more with white people and   make you more acceptable to them.

T/F 20. White women treat their men better than black women do.

T/F 21. Black people are more tolerant of differences than whites.

T/F 22. Black people are better off today than in the past.

T/F 23. Racial discrimination is a thing of the past.

T/F 24. Many of the problems blacks face are caused by blacks.

T/F 25. Black people are still struggling for freedom.

T/F 26. I disagree with most white people in general.

T/F 27. I feel uncomfortable when I am with all white people.

T/F 28. I am more comfortable when I am with all white people.

T/F 29. I feel that white people are smarter than black people.

T/F 30. I feel that black people fear white people.

T/F 31. I feel that white people would stay on a job longer than blacks.

T/F 32. I feel that white people work harder than black people.

T/F 33. I feel that white people do more for their people than black people theirs.

T/F 34. I believe that most white people would help me if they could.

T/F 35. I feel that white people can be trusted more than black people.

T/F 36. I feel that white people will always be in charge.

T/F 37. I want white people to be in charge of everything that black people do.

T/F 38. I believe that white people will tell black people how to raise their kids.

T/F 39. Black people see the world differently than whites.

T/F 40. I believe that white people can do things better than most blacks.

T/F 41. I believe Jesus was white.

T/F 42. I feel that only God has the answer to people's problems.

T/F 43. Black people are more religious than white people.

T/F 44. Black people commit more crimes than white people.

T/F 45. Teenagers who don't obey should be locked up.

T/F 46. I believe that money makes people equal.

T/F 47. I would rather live in a white community than a black community.

T/F 48. I feel that there is an advantage to being white in America.

T/F 49. Most white people are not prejudiced.

T/F 50. I believe that my vote is important.

T/F 51. Black people have the power to overcome discrimination.

T/F 52. Black people cause whites to discriminate against them.

T/F 53. I believe that everyone has equal opportunity in America.

T/F 54. I believe that there is a disadvantage to being black in America.

T/F 55. I feel that I can learn better from a white person than a black person.

T/F 56. I would rather have a white person as a friend than a black person.

T/F 57. Black people respect white people more than they respect other black people.

T/F 58. I believe that black people would rather be white than black.

T/F 59. Sometimes I wish I was another race.

T/F 60. I trust black people more than I trust whites.

T/F 61. I believe that I have achieved success because of the efforts of blacks who have   come before me.

T/F 62. I believe that knowledge of black history will help me become more successful.

Respondents are then asked to complete the following demographic information so that their responses may be compared by age, gender, religious orientation, and income.

1. Age: _____

2. Education:
   - Eighth grade or less
   - Some high school (What grade completed?_____)
   - High school graduate or GED
   - Some college
   - College graduate
   - Graduate or professional degree (What degree?_____)

3. Employment status:
   - a. Unemployed
   - b. Employed, full time
   - c. Employed, part time
   - d. Employed, disabled
   - e. Retired

4. Income:
- <$10,000 per year
- $10,000–$20,000
- $21,000–$39,999
- $40,000–$69,999
- $70,000–$79,999
- $80,000+

5. Gender:
- Male
- Female

6. Religious orientation:
- Protestant (Baptist, Presbyterian, etc.)
- Catholic
- Muslim
- Other (Please specify:_____)

References

Akbar, N. "Mental Disorders among African Americans." In *Black Psychology*, edited by R. L. Jones, 4, 339–352. Berkeley, CA: Cobb and Henry, 1991.

Akbar, N. *Chains and Images of Psychological Slavery*. Jersey City, NJ: New Mind Productions, 1990.

American Psychiatric Association. *Diagnostic and Statistical Manual of Mental Disorders*. 5th ed. Washington, DC: APA, 2013.

Arterburn, S. and J. Felton. *Toxic Faith*. Nashville, TN: Oliver-Nelson Books, 1991.

Blauner, Robert. *Racial Oppression in America*. New York: Harper and Row, 1972.

Booth, L. *When God Becomes a Drug*. Los Angeles: Tarcher, 1992.

Clark, K. B. *Dark Ghetto*. New York: Harper and Row, 1965.

Clark, K. B. and M. K. Clark. "Emotional Factors in Racial Identification and Preferences in Negro Children." *Journal of Negro Education*, no. 19 (1950): 341–350.

Clark, K. B. and M. K. Clark. "The Development of Self and the Emergence of Racial Identification in Negro Pre-School Children." *Journal of Social Psychology*, no. 10 (1939): 591–599.

Cone, J. H. *A Black Theology of Liberation*. Maryknoll, NY: Orbis Books, 1986.

Cone, J. H. *For My People: Black Theology and the Black Church.* Maryknoll, NY: Orbis Books, 1984.

Cosby, W. H. and A. F. Poussaint. *Come On, People: On the Path from Victims to Victors.* Nashville, TN: Thomas Nelson, 2007.

Cross, W. E. "Models of Psychological Nigressence: A Literature Review." In *Black Psychology*, edited by R. L. Jones, 2, 81–98. Berkeley, CA: Cobb and Henry, 1980.

Cross, W. E., T. A. Parham, and J. Helms. "The Stages of Black Identity Development: Nigrescence Models." In *Black Psychology*, 3rd ed., edited by R. L. Jones, 4, 319–338. Berkeley, CA: Cobb and Henry, 1991.

DuBois, W. E. B. (1903) 2007. *The Souls of Black Folk.* Reprint, New York: Oxford University Press.

Ellis, A. and Catharine MacLaren. *Rational Emotive Behavior Therapy: A Therapist's Guide.* Atascadero, CA: Impact Publishers, 1998.

Fanon, Frantz. *Black Skins, White Masks.* New York: Grove Press, 1967.

Fanon, Frantz. *The Wretched of the Earth.* New York: Grove Press, 1963.

Frazier, Franklin E. *The Negro Church in America.* Liverpool: University of Liverpool, 1963.

Gaston, A. G. *Green Power.* Troy, AL: Troy State University Press, 1968.

Grier, W. H. and P. M. Cobbs. *Black Rage.* New York: Basic Books, 1968.

Griffin, Q. D. and S. J. Korchin. "Personality Competence in Black Male Adolescents." *Journal of Youth and Adolescence* 9, no. 3 (1980): 211–227.

Guthrie, R. V. "The Psychology of Black Americans: An Historical Perspective." In *Black Psychology*, 2nd ed., edited by R. L. Jones, 1, 99–105. New York: Harper and Row, 1980.

Houston, L. "Black Consciousness and Self-Esteem." *Journal of Black Psychology* 11, no. 1 (1984): 1–7.

Jahoda, M. *Current Concepts of Positive Mental Health.* New York: Basic Books, 1958.

Jones, A. C. "Psychological Functioning in African Americans: A Conceptual Guide for Use in Psychotherapy." In *Black Psychology*, 3rd ed., edited by R. L. Jones. Berkeley, CA: Cobb and Henry, 1991.

Jones, J. M. "The Politics of Personality: Being Black in America." In *Black Psychology*, 3rd ed., edited by R. L. Jones, 4, 305–318. Berkeley, CA: Cobb and Henry, 1991.

Kambon, K. and Bowen-Reid, T. "Africentric Theories of African American Personality." In *Handbook of African American Psychology*, edited by H. Neville, B. Tynes, and S. Utsey, 61–74. Thousand Oaks, CA: Sage, 2009.

Kardiner, Abram and Lionel Ovesey. "On the Psychodynamics of the Negro Personality." In *The Self in Social Interaction*, edited by C. Gordon and K. Gergen, 24, 259–267. New York: John Wiley, 1968.

Kardiner, Abram and Lionel Ovesey. *The Mark of Oppression.* New York: Norton, 1951.

Karon, B. *The Negro Personality: A Rigorous Investigation of the Effects of the Culture.* New York: Springer, 1958.

King Jr., Gosby. *God's Prosperity: Obtaining Wealth God's Way*. Bloomington, IN: Authorhouse, 2003.

Kunjufu, J. *Countering the Conspiracy to Destroy Black Boys*. Chicago: African American Images, 1985.

Lincoln, C. Eric and Lawrence H. Mamiya. *The Black Church in the African American Experience*. Durham, NC: Duke University Press, 1990.

Love, P. and J. Robinson. *The Emotional Incest Syndrome*. New York: Bantam Books, 1990.

Malcolm X, with Alex Haley. (1965) 1990. *The Autobiography of Malcolm X*. Reprint, New York: Ballantine Books.

Monihan, D. *The Negro Family: The Case for National Action*. Washington, DC: US Department of Labor, 1965.

Mosby, D. P. "Toward a Theory of the Unique Personality of Blacks." In *Black Psychology*, edited by R. L. Jones, 124–135. New York: Harper and Row, 1972.

Mosby, D. P. "Toward a New Specialty of Black Psychology." In *Black Psychology*, 2nd ed., edited by R. L. Jones, 2, 295–304. Berkeley, CA: Cobb and Henry, 1980.

Nobles, W. N. "Extended Self: Rethinking the So-Called Negro Self-Concept." In *Black Psychology*, edited by R. L. Jones, 99–105. Berkley: Cobb and Henry, 1991.

Parker Jr., J. *Holy Change: A Systematic Approach to Transforming a Community*. Bloomington, IN: Author Solutions, 2008.

Poussaint, A. F. *Why Blacks Kill Blacks*. New York: Emerson Hall, 1972.

Ramseur, H. P. "Psychologically Healthy Black Adults." In *Black Psychology*, 3rd ed., edited by R. L. Jones, 4, 353–378, Berkeley, CA: Cobb and Henry, 1991.

Reed, Gregory J. *Economic Empowerment through the Church.* Grand Rapids, MI: Zaondervan, 1994.

Stampp, K. M. *The Peculiar Institution: Slavery in the Ante-Bellum South.* New York: Vintage Books, 1956.

Thomas, A. and S. Sillen. *Racism and Psychiatry.* New York: Brunner/Mazel, 1972.

Vanderheyden, P. A. "Religious Addiction: The Subtle Destruction of the Soul." *Pastoral Psychology* 47, no. 4 (1999): 293–302.

Washington, Booker T. "The Atlanta Compromise Speech." In *The Booker T. Washington Papers*, 1974, vol. 3, edited by L. R. Harlin, 583–587. Urbana: University of Illinois Press, 1865.

White, J. "Toward a Black Psychology." In *Black Psychology*, edited by R. L. Jones, 43–50. New York: Harper and Row Publishers, 1972.

Washington, Booker T. *A New Negro for a New Century.* Chicago: American Publishing House, 1900.

Washington, Booker T. *Up from Slavery.* New York: Doubleday, 1901.

Williams, R. L. *The Collective Black Mind: An Afro-Centric Theory of Black Personality.* Saint Louis: Williams and Associates, 1981.

Williams, Twyla J. *Save Our Children: The Struggle between Black Parents and Schools.* Houston: Williams, 2009.

Woodson, Carter G. (1933) 1969. *The Mis-Education of the Negro.* Reprint, Washington DC: Associated Publishers.

Wright, B. *The Psychopathic Racial Personality*. Chicago: Third World Press, 1975.

Recommended Reading List

Bennett Jr., Lerone. *Black Power USA*. Baltimore: Penguin Books, 1967.

Bennett Jr., Lerone. *Before the* Mayflower*: A History of the Negro in America*. Chicago: Johnson Publishing, 1966.

Boyd-Franklin, Nancy. *Black Families in Therapy*. New York: Guilford Press, 2003.

Brown, Robert. *Manchild in the Promised Land*. New York: Macmillan, 1965.

Butler, John S. *Entrepreneurship and Self-Help among Black Americans*. New York: State University of New York Press, 1991.

Clark, Kenneth B. *Dark Ghetto: Dilemmas of Social Power*. New York: Harper and Row, 1965.

Comer, James P. *Beyond Black and White*. New York: Quadrangle Books, 1972.

Comer, J. P. and A. F. Poussaint. *Raising Black Children: Two Leading Psychiatrists Confront the Educational, Social and Emotional Problems Facing Black Children*. New York: Penguin Books, 1992.

Cosby, Bill. *Fatherhood*. New York: Doubleday, 1986.

Craig, Russell. *The Socio-Economic Truth of Black America*. Decatur, GA: Remnant Publishing, 1992.

Cruse, Harold. *The Crisis of the Negro Intellectual*. New York: William Morrow and Company, 1967.

Douglass, Frederick. *The Narrative of the Life of Frederick Douglass*. New York: Dover, 1845.

Dryden, Charles W. *A-Train: Memoirs of a Tuskegee Airman*. Tuscaloosa: University of Alabama Press, 1997.

DuBois, W. E. B. (1903) 2007. *The Souls of Black Folk*. Reprint, New York: Oxford University Press.

Dyson, Eric M. *I May Not Get There with You: The True Martin Luther King, Jr*. New York: The Free Press, 2000.

Ellison, Ralph. *Invisible Man*. New York: Vintage, 1947.

Fanon, Frantz. *Black Skins, White Masks*. New York: Grove Press, 1967.

Fanon, Frantz. *The Wretched of the Earth*. New York: Grove Press, 1963.

Frazier, E. Franklin. *The Negro Church in America*. Liverpool: University of Liverpool, 1963.

Frazier, E. Franklin. *Black Bourgeoisie*. New York: The Free Press, 1957.

Frazier, Thomas R. *Afro-American History Primary Sources*. New York: Harcourt, Brace & World, 1970.

Gates, Henry Louis. *Thirteen Ways of Looking at a Black Man*. New York: Random House, 1997.

Gates, Henry Louis. *The African-American Century: How Black Americans Have Shaped Our Century*. New York: Free Press, 2000.

Gates, H. L. and D. Yacavone. *The African Americans: Many Rivers to Cross*. New York: SmileyBooks, 2013.

Gates, Henry Louis. *Life upon These Shores: Looking at African American History, 1513–2008*. New York: Knopf Doubleday, 2011.

Greenberg, Kenneth S. *Nat Turner*. New York: Oxford University Press, 2003.

Griffin, Howard J. *Black Like Me*. New York: Signet, 1960.

Hare, N. *Black Anglo-Saxons*. New York: Mangani and Morrell, 1965.

Henderson Jr., Perry E. *The Black Church Credit Union*. Lima, OH: Fairway Press, 1990.

Hopson, D. P. and D. S. Hopson. *The Power of Soul*. New York: William Morrow, 1998.

Jordan, Winthrop D. *The White Man's Burden*. New York: Oxford University Press, 1974.

Kremer, Gary R. *George Washington Carver: In His Own Words*. Columbia: University of Missouri Press, 1987.

Lander, Joyce A. *The Death of White Sociology*. New York: Random House, 1973.

Lander, J. and T. F. DiGeronimo. *Launching Our Black Children for Success: A Guide for Parents of Kids from Three to Eighteen*. San Francisco: Jossey-Bass, 2003.

Lewis, Reginald F. and S. Walker Blair. *Why Should White Guys Have All the Fun?* New York: Wiley & Sons, 1995.

McMurry, Linda O. *George Washington Carver: Scientist and Symbol*. New York: Oxford University Press, 1981.

Nobles, W. W. "African Philosophy: Foundations of Black Psychology." In *Black Psychology*, 3rd ed., edited by R. L. Jones, 4, 47–63. Berkeley, CA: Cobb and Henry, 1991.

Obama, Barack. *Dreams from My Father*. New York: Three Rivers Press, 1995.

Patterson, H. and E. Conrad. *Scottsboro Boy*. New York: Bantam, 1950.

Pinderhughes, Elaine. *Understanding Race, Ethnicity, and Power*. New York: The Free Press, 1989.

Poussaint, A. F. and A. Alexander. *Lay My Burdens Down: Unraveling Suicide and Mental Health Crisis among African-Americans*. Boston: Beacon Press, 2000.

Quarles, Benjamin. *The Negro in the Making of America*. New York: Macmillan, 1964.

Robbins, Anthony, and Joseph McClendon. *Unlimited Power: A Black Choice*. New York: Simon & Schuster, 1997.

Robinson, Randall. *The Reckoning*. New York: Penguin, 2002.

Robinson, Randall. *The Debt*. New York: Plume, 2001.

Rogers, C. R. *On Becoming a Person: A Therapist's View of Psychotherapy*. Boston: Houghton Mifflin, 1961.

Smiley, Tavis. *The Covenant*. Chicago: Third World Press, 2006.

Taylor, Kristin C. *Black Fathers*. New York: Doubleday, 2003.

Truth, Sojourner. (1850) 1997. *Narrative of Sojourner Truth*. Reprint, New York: Dover.

West, C. *Race Matters*. Boston: Beacon Press, 1993.

Williams, Chancellor. *The Destruction of African Civilization.* Chicago: Third World Press, 1974.

Williams, Richard. *They Stole It but You Must Return It.* New York: HEMA Publishing, 1991.

Woodward, C. Vann. *The Strange Career of Jim Crow.* New York: Oxford University Press, 1966.

Wright, Richard. *Black Boy.* New York: Harper and Row, 1937.

Yett, Samuel F. *The Choice.* Silver Spring, MD: Cottage Books, 1971.

Young, Andrew. *An Easy Burden.* New York: HarperCollins Publishers, 1996.

Recommended Video References

4 Little Girls. 1997. New York: Home Box Office Studio Productions.

Africans in America. 1998. WGBH Boston Video. WGBH Educational Foundation.

Amistad. 1999. Universal City, CA: DreamWorks LLC.

Marcus Garvey. 2001. WGBH Educational Foundation. PBS Home Video.

Mighty Times: The Legacy of Rosa Parks. 2002. Montgomery, AL: Southern Poverty Law Center.

A Remembrance of Martin. 1986. Dallas, TX: IDANHA Films. PBS Home Video.

A Time for Justice. 1992. Montgomery, AL: Charles Guggenheim Southern Poverty Law Center.

The Tuskegee Airmen. 1995. New York: Home Box Office Studio Productions.

Unforgivable Blackness: The Rise and Fall of Jack Johnson. 2004. The American Lines II Film Project. PBS Home Video.

X: Malcolm X. 1992. Burbank, CA: Warner Brothers Home Video.

Gates, H. L. 2004. *America Beyond the Color Line*. BBC2/PBS.

Gates, H. L. 2012. *Finding Your Roots with Henry Louis Gates Jr.* PBS.

Gates, H. L. 2013. *The African Americans: Many Rivers to Cross.* PBS.

Gates, H. L. 2011. *Black in Latin America.* PBS.